바로 쓸 수 있는 비즈니스 영작문

HANDY ENGLISH WRITING FOR BUSINESS

황남엽 지음

신아사

이 연구는 2022년도 협성대학교 교내 연구비 지원에 의한 연구임(2022-0026).

머리말

책을 마무리하며 뒤돌아보니 생각보다 많은 시간과 노력이 녹아 들어갔다. 몇 해 전 4학년 학생들을 대상으로 하는 <비즈니스 영작문> 과목을 맡게 되면서부터 초안구성을 시작하여 이제야 탈고를 하게 되었으니 꼬박 2년이 넘게 걸린 셈이다. 힘든 여정이었지만 그럼에도 불구하고 이 책의 필요성을 절감했던 것은 기존의 대다수 비즈니스 영작문 교재들이 영작보다는 비즈니스 영어에만 초점을 맞추고 있었기 때문이다. 영작을 할 만한 공간도 충분히 제공하지 않았고 내용도 어려웠다. 책 속에 갇힌 비즈니스 영어를 작문을 통해 살아 있는 영어로 만들고 싶은 '욕망' 이 발동했다. 이 문제를 풀어가는 과정에서 주목했던 것은 현재 서구권에서 사용하고 있는 영문 비즈니스 레터, 이메일 나아가 팩스 보내는 양식을 보다 정확하게 제공하고, 이를 토대로 학생들로 하여금 다양한 비즈니스 관련 문장을 직접 쓰도록 안내함으로써 그야말로 영어문장을 바로 쓸 수 있도록 한 것이다. 그리고 영작을 하는 과정에서 드러나는 자신의 크고 작은 실수를 통해 영어를 습득하게 하고, 문장이 아닌 문맥을 통해서 단어와 구(phrase) 그리고 문장을 배우고 익혀가도록 한 것이 이 책의 특징이라 할 수 있다.

이 책은 비즈니스 영작문 저서임에도 불구하고 국문 자기소개서와 이력서로 시작한다. 비즈니스 문서의 첫 단계라고 할 수 있는 영문 자기소개서와 이력서를 소개하기 전에 국문 자기소개서와 이력서를 삽입한 것은 학생들이 각각의 작성방식에서 드러나는 차이를 직접 경험하고 느껴보기를 바라는 필자의 소망 때문이다. 이것은 작성방식에서의 기술적인 차이를 초월한, 어쩌면 서양과 동양의 문화와 인식에서 드러나는 미묘한 차이인 동시에 한국식 문법내용과 미국식 영작과정에서 생겨나는 다양한 오류들에 대한 고민이기도 하다. 특히 영어실력의 차이가 나는 두 학생의 영문 자기소개서 내용을 그대로 수록함으로써 그들의 실수를 다시 수정하고 자신의 문장으로 다시 써보게 하는 공간을 마련하였고, 이어지는 교수자의 정답에 대한 설명과 더불어 '원어민이 보기에 바람직한 문장이 무엇인가?'에 대해 고민을 하게 하였다. 이 책에서는 원어민이 보기에 완벽한 문장을 (O)으로, 문법적으로 올바르지만 어색한 문장으로 간주되는 문장을 (△)로, 그리고 완벽하게 틀린 문장을 (X)로 표시했다. 또한 필요한 경우, 원어민의 설명을 그대로 첨부하여 가급적 원어민의 시각으로 문장을 바라보는 힘을 키우도록 하였다. 한국인의 시각에서 벗어난, 영어문장에 대한 고민의 장이 학생들에게 영작의 힘을 키우는 밑거름이 될 것으로 믿는다. 영원히 부족할 수밖에 없는 내용이지만 이러한 나의 새로운 시도가 대학 4학년 학생들, 취업준비를 하는 예비직장인들 그리고 사회생활을 하면서 영작에 관심이 있는 모든 이들에게 도움이 되기를 바란다. 마지막으로 출판을 허락해주신 신아사의 정현걸 사장님과 멀리 떨어진 캐나다에서 많은 도움을 준 오랜 친구, Winnie Mah에게 특별히 감사의 마음을 전한다.

I'd like to say 'thank you' to my friend, Winnie, for her continued help and encouragement. She is a valued friend, for which I am grateful.

2022년 10월

황남엽

Contents

Capitalization Rules[1]

1. At the beginning of each sentence, the first word is always capitalized.

He goes to the movies twice a week.

They accepted my advice.

2. The personal pronoun I is always capitalized.

Jae and **I** are the cousins' brothers.

3. Professional and formal titles begin with capital letters.

Mary had an appointment with **Dr**. Im at his dental clinic yesterday.

Mr. Kim is a janitor at school.

4. Proper nouns (specific people and places) begin with capital letters.

She is going to do a family trip to **V**ancouver **I**sland.

I met **W**innie in the class titled Asian Canadian Literature at SFU.

(= I met **W**innie at SFU in the class Asian Canadian Literature.)

5. Names of streets and avenues are capitalized.

The restaurant is on **L**ombard **S**treet.

She lives on **C**ape **H**orn **A**ve.

6. Countries, states, cities, continents, rivers, and lakes begin with capital letters.

My mon and I visited **I**taly last winter for one week.

What time does the train for **P**usan leave?

The bridge was built over the **H**an **R**iver when I was young.

7. The names of nationalities and languages begin with capital letters.

Bethany is **C**anadian but Mary Grace is **K**orean.

My friend speaks **E**nglish.

1) 이 책에 실린 rules들은 본인이 저술한 『준동사로 영작문 뽀개기』(동인출판사, 2018)를 저본으로 하였다.

8. The titles of books, essays, newspapers, and magazines are capitalized, that is, the first letters of titles are always capitalized: Do not capitalize conjunctions (but, and), articles (a, an, the), or prepositions (from, to, in) unless they are the first word of the titles.

Jane **E**yre — the title of book

The **V**ancouver **S**un — the title of newspaper

People — the title of magazine

9. Specific course names begin with capital letters.

They are taking **H**istory 107 at noon.

They took history last semester. — general subject does not begin with capital letter

Comma Rules

1. Put a comma before conjunctions (but, and, or, nor, so, yet) when they connect two simple sentences.

Jennifer bought Nolan a toy, but he disliked it.

2. Place a comma between three or more items in a series.

Grace brought an umbrella, a towel, and a brush to the beach.

3. Put a comma after a subordinate clause when the clause begins a sentence.

Because we missed the subway last night, we couldn't arrive on time.

= We couldn't arrive on time because we missed the subway last night.

4. Commas are used to separate the day from the date, and the date from the year. Separate a city and state with commas.

He was born on Monday, March 15, 2000.

The conference was held in Incheon, Korea.

5. When using introductory words or phrases, a comma is used to separate them from the main sentence.

Finally, I passed the English exam.

Every morning, I get up early and exercise in the gym. (0)

= Every morning, I get up early to exercise in the gym. (00)

6. A comma is used to separate unnecessary information in a sentence.

Seoul, which is the capital of Korea, has a lot of pollution.

William Shakespeare, the most famous writer in the Age of Neo-Classicism, wrote *Macbeth*.

7. Place a comma after the salutation and the closing of personal letters.

Dear Winnie, With love, Mary Grace	Dear Mrs. Macbeth, Sincerely, Jonathan	Dear Dr. Park, Yours truly, Alice

Spelling Rules for Regular Verbs and Plural Nouns

1. Add -s to most verbs and to most nouns.

swim	swims
like	likes
work	works
desk	desks
pen	pens

2. If a verb or noun ends with ch, sh, s, x, z, then add -es.

church	churches
push	pushes
box	boxes
bus	buses
buzz	buzzes

3. If a verb or noun ends with a consonant + y, then change y to -ies.

study	studies
party	parties
city	cities

4. If a verb or noun ends with a vowel + y, then add -s.

buy	buys
boy	boys
monkey	monkeys

5. If a verb or noun ends with -o, then add -es.

tomato	tomatoes
go	goes
mango	mangoes

Spelling Rules for Regular Past Tense Verbs

1. Add -ed to most verbs.

start	started
work	worked
obtain	obtained

2. When the verb ends with -e, then add -d.

like	liked
care	cared
change	changed

3. If a verb ends with a consonant + y, then change the -y to -ied.

study	studied
satisfy	satisfied
try	tried

4. If a verb ends with a vowel + y, then just add -ed.

stay	stayed
play	played
destroy	destroyed
enjoy	enjoyed

5. For words containing one syllable and ending in a consonant + vowel + consonant (CVC), double the final consonant when adding -ed.

stop	stopped
plan	planned
beg	begged

6. In the case of two syllable words ending in CVC, of which the second syllable is stressed, the final consonant is doubled when adding -ed.

occur	occurred
permit	permitted
commit	committed
omit	omitted

Spelling of the -ing

1. Add -ing to most verbs.

wear	wearing
study	studying
spend	spending

2. For verbs ending in a (consonant + -e), drop the -e before adding -ing.

write	writing
move	moving
live	living

3. In the case of one syllable verbs ending in a consonant + vowel + consonant (CVC), double the final consonant before adding -ing.

run	running
swim	swimming
stop	stopping

4. For two syllable verbs ending in CVC, of which the second syllable is also stressed, the final consonant is doubled before adding -ing.

begin	beginning
submit	submitting
refer	referring
confer	conferring

5. When the first syllable is stressed in a two syllable verb ending in CVC, the final consonant is not doubled when adding -ing.

open	opening
visit	visiting
limit	limiting

Spelling Exceptions for A and An

When choosing between using the words "a" or "an" before a word, take note if the word begins with a vowel. "A" is used before a word that begins with a consonant. "An" is used before a word beginning with a vowel. The letters "h" and "u" have exceptions.

① Words Begins with *H*

When words begin with a pronounced "*h*", use "a".	a horse a hat a hater a hot dog
When words begin with a silent "*h*", use "an".	an hour an herb an honest man an heir

② Words Begins with *U*

When *u* is pronounced like "uh", use "an"	an umbrella an umpire
When the *u* is pronounced like "you", use "a"	a university a uniform

Fundamental Exercises

** 다음 문장을 읽고 틀린 부분을 올바르게 수정하여 전체 문장을 다시 쓰시오.

1. Lake louise in Canada is a beautiful place to visit.

→ ______________________________

2. Tom is Korean but Jane is japanese.

→ ______________________________

3. they will bring a pen, a bottle of water and an eraser.

→ ______________________________

4. I was born on saturday May 15th, 1966.

→ ______________________________

5. We studyed English very hard last night.

→ ______________________________

6. The teacher visited many church yesterday.

→ ______________________________

7. that boy go to the mountain every morning.

→ ______________________________

8. There are many bus on the street.

→ ______________________________

9. I went to the city, incheon a few years ago, but from now on I will try to visit many city.

→ ____

____

10. I saw many monkey at the zoo in india.

→ ____

11. They brought some fruits, a apple and a few mangos.

→ ____

11-① I ate breakfast drank tea and washed the dishes.

→ ____

12. The coworker met a honest and pretty lady.

→ ____

13. The janitor left a umbrella in his car.

→ ____

14. The professor is writeing a letter to his friend in France.

→ ____

15. That leaf growing in this garden is a herb.

→ ____

16. My colleague was satisfyed with the result of the report.

→ ____

17. Jeniffer stoped working at this restaurant as a part-time job.

→ ______________________________

18. The secretary omited to copy the back page of the newspaper.

→ ______________________________

19. Today is in March 1, 2022.

→ ______________________________

20. When I go to work I prefer taking public transportation.

→ ______________________________

1장

국문 자기소개서

예전에는 취업준비생이 자신이 원하는 회사에 자기소개서를 제출할 때 일종의 표준화된 자기소개서 양식을 참고하여 작성하였다. 그러나 요즘에는 각 회사가 제공하고 있는 여러 형태의 온라인 국문 자기소개서 양식이 있기 때문에 본인이 취업하고자 하는 특정 회사 양식에 맞추어 자기소개서 및 이력서를 작성해야 한다. 이때 간과해서는 안 될 것이 비슷비슷한 자기소개서 중에서 남과 다른 <나>를 가장 잘 어필할 수 있으면서 이와 동시에 기업의 인재상에 부합할 수 있는 자기소개서를 작성해야 한다는 점이다.

'나'를 어필할 수 있는 방법으로 유의해야 할 점은 공모전 수상, 대기업 인턴과 같은 사회의 객관적 기준을 바탕으로 자신을 부각시키는 것보다는 본인의 주관적인 가치기준을 바탕으로 자신과 회사 그리고 직무에 대한 연결고리를 자신만의 독특한 생각과 언어로 표현할 수 있어야 한다는 것이다. 외부에서 강요당한 스펙 위주의 일반적이고도 표준화된 자기소개서의 내용이 아니라 나만의 독특하고도 진솔한 스토리를 들려줌으로써 다른 지원자와 다른 자신만의 차별점을 보여주는 것이 바람직하다. 예를 들어 스펙 쌓기에 투자하는 시간을 좀 줄이고 직접 실무자를 만나 관련 직무에 관한 조언을 구한다던지, 지원하고자 하는 회사의 사업장이나 매장을 방문함으로써 기업에 대한 관심과 직무에 대한 자신만의 노력을 어필할 수도 있다.

또한 성장배경 혹은 가정환경과 같은 구태의연한 가족관계 내용은 최소한으로 줄이고 자신이 회사에 부합한 인재라는 것을 부각시켜야 할 필요가 있다. 기업은 소위 똑똑한 인재를 단순히 선발하려고 하는 것이 아니라 회사의 이윤창출을 위한 지원자의 적합성 유무를 따지면서 조직구성원으로서 '함께 갈 사람'을 뽑으려고 하기 때문이다. 따라서 기업에 대한 배경지식을 바탕으로 자신이 기업에 맞는 인재상이라는 것을 어필하면서 조직원으로서 협업이 뛰어나고 동시에 업무에 대해서도 남다른 관심과 열정을 가지고 있다는 것을 자신의 과업을 통해 피력해야 한다. 다시 말해 회사에서 필요로 하는 업무에 자신이 어떤 강점을 가지고 있는지를 나타내는 것이 우선시 되어야 한다고 볼 수 있다.

자기소개서를 작성하는 기술과 관련해서, 쓰고자 하는 내용의 우선순위를 고려한 후 질문에 대한 답변을 먼저 보여주는 두괄식이 바람직하며, 항목별 소제목을 달아줌으로써 해당 항목에서 자신이 쓰고자 하는 내용을 간략하게 표현하는 것이 좋다. 문장은 간결해야 하며 주장하고자 하는 내용에 있어서는 그것을 뒷받침하는 구체적인 사례도 함께 적는 것을 추천한다. 또한 부각하고자 하는 내용을 다양한 색깔이나 폰트를 사용하여 지나치게 강조하기보다는 전체적으로 통일성을 고려하여 작성하는 것이 바람직하다.

Part 1. 국문 자기소개서 양식

국문 자기소개서의 모든 항목들은 지원하는 회사 및 분야에 연관되기 때문에 내가 아닌 '회사'의 관점에서 자기소개서를 작성해야 한다. 일반적으로 자기소개서에는 성장과정, 성격의 장 단점, 생활태도, 인생관, 경력사항 및 현장경험, 지원동기 등의 6가지로 이루어진다. 회사에 따라 추가되는 항목이 있을 수 있지만 위에서 언급한 6가지 항목이 주된 내용이라 할 수 있다.

<자기소개서>

■ 인적사항

성 명		성별	□ 남 □ 여	생년월일	
주 소					
최종학교	(대학교 / 전문대 / 고등학교)			전 공	

■ 자기소개서

성장과정	
성격의 장단점	
생활태도	
인생관	
경력사항 및 현장경험 (실습, 자원봉사 포함)	
지원동기	

1. 성장과정

성장과정을 기술하는 것은 가족관계나 가정환경과 같은 객관적인 사실을 적는 것이 아니라 자신의 삶 깊숙이 자리 잡은 철학이나 행동방식 등을 서술하는 것이다. 특히 어린 시절에 대한 서술은 인사담당자에게 강한 인상을 남길 수 있는 요소가 되기 때문에 에피소드 형식으로 기술하는 것이 좋은데, 이때 지나치게 감정적인 어조로 서술하는 것을 지양해야 한다. 자신의 인생에 영향을 끼친 인물이나 인상 깊게 읽은 책에 대해서도 언급할 수 있다.

2. 성격의 장단점

지원자의 성격은 장차 회사생활에서 접하게 될 다양한 업무상황에서 성과를 결정짓는 중요한 기본자질이 된다. 따라서 지원자는 자신의 성격을 추상적으로 쓰지 말고 명확하게 기술해야한다. 단점의 경우, 자신이 단점을 어떻게 극복했고 그러한 노력의 결과가 무엇이었는지에 대해 구체적으로 적는다. 또한 장점의 경우에도, 자신의 성격을 명확하게 기술할 수 있는 구체적인 근거를 통해 자신의 장점을 겸손하면서도 자신을 드러낼 수 있는 당당한 어조로 작성한다.

3. 생활태도

인간은 말이나 글보다는 실생활 속에서 자신의 진실한 모습을 보여준다. 생활 속에서 접하게 되는 특별한 경험이나 반복되는 행동양식은 자신이 가지고 있는 가치관과 능력을 나타내는 좋은 계기가 되기 때문이다. 따라서 글이나 말로 표현하는 자소서나 면접의 한계를 뛰어넘어 자신이 실생활에서 경험했던 내용을 간단하게 전달하는 것도 상대방에서 뚜렷한 인상을 남길 수 있다.

4. 인생관

사회에 진출하려는 청년층을 대상으로 어떤 것에 가치를 두고 생활해 왔는지 나아가 세상을 바라보는 관점이 무엇인지를 묻는 경우가 종종 있다. 이때 유의할 것은 과장되거나 추상적인 말로 중언부언하기 보다는 두괄식으로 강조하고자 하는 좌우명을 짧게 적고, 이에 대한 설명을 간결하게 덧붙일 것을 권장한다.

5. 경력사항 및 현장경험 (실습, 자원봉사 포함)

경력사항 및 현장경험은 자기소개서의 꽃이라고 할 수 있는 가장 중요한 항목이다. 회사는 이윤 창출을 위해 지원자가 얼마나 효율적으로 업무성과를 실현시킬 수 있는지에 대한 잠재력을 보고 싶어 한다. 따라서 현장경험을 통한 자신의 경력과 강점을 단순히 나열하기 보다는 업무성과 위주로, 다시 말해 자신이 어떤 결과를 만들어 냈는지에 대해 구체적으로 언급함으로써 자신이 회사에 부합한 인재하는 것을 증명할 필요가 있다.

6. 지원동기

입사지원 동기는 (경력사항 및 현장경험과 더불어) 자기소개서에서 매우 중요한 비중을 차지한다. '채용해주시면 열심히 일하겠습니다'라는 진부한 표현이 아니라 적극적이고도 구체적인 입사지원 동기를 밝혀야 한다. 예를 들면, 자신이 지원하고자 하는 기업에 얼마나 많은 관심과 열의를 가지고 입사를 위해 해당직무와 관련하여 무엇을 준비해 왔는지 기술해야 하며, 자신의 역량과 비전을 회사의 경영철학이라든지 인재상 등과 비교한 후, 서로간의 연결점을 찾아 보다 설득력 있게 입사지원동기를 밝히는 것이 좋다.

2장

영문 자기소개서 작성 사례

Warm up:

영문 자기소개서(Cover Letter)에 대한 설명을 본격적으로 시작하기 전에 일종의 준비운동으로서 소위 영어실력이 부족한, A 학생이 작성한 영문 자기소개서와 영어실력이 뛰어난, B 학생이 작성한 영문 자기소개서 내용을 수정 전과 후로 나누어 기재하였다. 그리고 그 과정에서 드러나는 그들의 실수를 토대로 오류가 있는 잘못된 문장을 올바른 문장으로 다시 수정하는 훈련의 장을 마련하였다.

Part 1. A 학생의 영문 자기소개서

hi my name is kim nam yeob my major is Department of chinese. I grew up under my parents who didn't put much pressure on me to study. My advantage is to do things that have to be done before the time period, So I do most of the work on time without delay. To be honest, I chose chinese because I had to go on to college. I didn't have anything I wanted to do at the time. when I was in second grade in the high school, I chose to take a second foreign language class. Later, I became interested in Chinese after my mother recommended a Chinese language academy. So I chose an university department related to China. Last year, I went to Taiwan with my friend. My friend wasn't good at Chinese, so I was almost in charge of Chinese. As I was in contact with Chinese at restaurants and tourist attractions, It was not easy to speak Chinese, but it was fun to talk in Chinese. And when I was in my first year of college, I joined an international exchange network. I felt it was fun to talk and interact with foreign friends. So I would like to have a job related to Chinese language.

Part 2 해석

안녕하세요 제 이름은 김남엽이고 제 전공은 중국어과입니다. 저는 저에게 공부하라고 많은 부담을 주지 않으셨던 부모님 밑에서 성장했습니다. 제 장점은 기한 전에 마쳐야 할 일들을 해내는 것입니다. 그래서 저는 대부분의 일들을 지체없이 제 시간에 해냅니다. 솔직히 말하면 제가 중국어를 선택한 이유는 대학에 진학하기 위해서였습니다. 그 당시 저는 하고 싶었던 것이 아무 것도 없었습니다. 고등학교 2학년 때, (저는) 제2외국어 수업을 받기로 선택했습니다. 얼마 후, 어머니께서 중국어학원을 추천해 주신 후에 (저는) 중국어에 관심을 가지게 되었습니다. 그래서 저는 중국과 관련된 대학 학과를 선택했습니다. 작년에, 저는 친구와 함께 대만에 갔습니다. 제 친구는 중국어를 잘하지 못해서 제가 거의 중국어를 담당했습니다. (제가) 식당과 관광명소에서 중국인과 만났을 때, 중국어로 말하는 것이 쉽지 않았지만 중국어로 이야기하는 것은 재미있었습니다. 그리고 대학교 1학년 때, (저는) 국제교류모임에 가입했습니다. 외국인 친구들과 대화하고 교류하는 것은 즐겁다고 생각했습니다. 그래서 저는 중국어와 관련된 직장을 얻고 싶습니다.

<English words and idioms>

grow up under ~의 밑에서 성장하다. ~의 밑에서 자라다
put pressure[1] on ~에게 부담을 주다, ~에게 압박을 가하다,
time period 기한
on time 제 시간에, 정각에, 시간을 어기지 않고
without delay 지체 없이, 신속히, 연기하지 않고
to be honest 솔직히 말하자면, 솔직히 말해서
go on to college 대학에 진학하다 = go to college
at the time 그 당시, 그 때, 그 즈음
(in) the second grade in high school 고등학교 2학년 (△)
second foreign language 제2외국어
take a class 수업을 받다
Chinese language academy 중국어학원
good at ~에 능숙한, ~을 잘하는
in charge of ~을 맡아서, ~을 담당해서
in contact with ~와 만나다. ~와 연락하다
tourist attractions 관광명소
international exchange network 국제교류모임

1) 영어 단어 스펠링에 밑줄을 친 것은 그곳에 강세가 있다는 것을 의미한다.

Part 3 영작연습

다음 문장을 올바르게 수정하시오.

1. hi my name is kim nam yeob my major is Department of chinese.
(안녕하세요 제 이름은 김남엽이고 제 전공은 중국어과입니다.)

→ ______________________________

2. I grew up under my parents who didn't put much pressure on me to study.
(저는 저에게 공부하라고 많은 부담을 주지 않으셨던 부모님 밑에서 성장했습니다.)

→ ______________________________

<grow up under / put pressure on>

3. My advantage is to do things that have to be done before the time period,
(제 장점은 기한 전에 마쳐야 할 일들을 해내는 것입니다.)

→ ______________________________

<time period>

4. So I do most of the work on time without delay.
(그래서 저는 대부분의 일들을 지체없이 제 시간에 해냅니다.)

→ ______________________________

<on time / without delay>

5. To be honest, I chose chinese because I had to go on to college.
(솔직히 말하면 제가 중국어를 선택한 이유는 대학에 진학하기 위해서였습니다.)

→ ______________________________

<to be honest / go on to college>

6. I didn't have anything I wanted to do at the time.
(그 당시 저는 하고 싶었던 것이 아무 것도 없었습니다.)

→ ______________________________

<at the time>

7. when I was in second grade in the high school, I chose to take a second foreign language class.

(고등학교 2학년 때, (저는) 제2외국어 수업을 받기로 선택했습니다.)

→ ____

____

< second foreign language / take a class>

8. Later, I became interested in Chinese after my mother recommended a Chinese language academy.

(얼마 후, 어머니께서 중국어학원을 추천해 주신 후에 (저는) 중국어에 관심을 가지게 되었습니다.)

→ ____

____

<Chinese language academy>

9. So I chose an university department related to China.

(그래서 저는 중국과 관련된 대학 학과를 선택했습니다.)

→ ____

10. Last year, I went to Taiwan with my friend.

(작년에, 저는 친구와 함께 대만에 갔습니다.)

→ ____

11. My friend wasn't good at Chinese, so I was almost in charge of Chinese.

(제 친구는 중국어를 잘하지 못해서 제가 거의 중국어를 담당했습니다.)

→ ____

<good at / in charge of>

12. As I was in contact with Chinese at restaurants and tourist attractions, It was not easy to speak Chinese, but it was fun to talk in Chinese.

(제가 식당과 관광명소에서 중국인과 만났을 때, 중국어로 말하는 것이 쉽지 않았지만 중국어로 이야기하는 것은 재미있었습니다.)

→ ____

____

<in contact with / tourist attractions>

13. And when I was in my first year of college, I joined an international exchange network.
(그리고 대학교 1학년 때, (저는) 국제교류모임에 가입했습니다.)

→ ____

14. I felt it was fun to talk and interact with foreign friends.
(외국인 친구들과 대화하고 교류하는 것은 즐겁다고 생각했습니다.)

→ ____

15. So I would like to have a job related to Chinese language.
(그래서 저는 중국어와 관련된 직장을 얻고 싶습니다.)

→ ____

Part 4 정답과 해설

<English Words and Idioms>

be proficient in/with ~을 잘하다, ~에 능숙하다 (= be efficient in/with)
time-management 시간관리
university department 대학 학과
almost always 대부분
interact 소통하다. 교류하다. = be in contact with

1. hi my name is kim nam yeob my major is Department of chinese.
(안녕하세요 제 이름은 김남엽이고 제 전공은 중국어과입니다.)

→ **Hello,** my name is **Kim, Namyeob,** and my major is **Chinese.**
= Hello, my name is Kim, Namyeob**,** and **I major in** Chinese.

2. I grew up under my parents who didn't put much pressure on me to study.
(저는 저에게 공부하라고 많은 부담을 주지 않으셨던 부모님 밑에서 성장했습니다.)
<grow up under / put pressure on>

→ I grew up under my parents**, who** did not put much pressure on me to study.
* <... **, who**>는 관계대명사의 계속적 용법으로서 해석은 앞에서부터 한다: 저는 부모님 밑에서 성장했는데 부모님께서는 제게 공부하라고 많은 부담을 주지 않으셨습니다>

3. My advantage is to do things that have to be done before the time period,
(제 장점은 기한 전에 마쳐야 할 일들을 해내는 것입니다.)
<time period>

* 장점에 해당하는 영어단어는 'advantage', 'strong point', 'strength', 'merit'이다. 그러나 이 문맥에서 단순히 'advantage'를 사용하면 어색한 문장이 되기 때문에 'be proficient in'이나 'be proficient with'로 바꾸어 수정해야 한다:

→ I **am proficient in** time-management, and completing tasks when they are assigned to me[2].
= I **am proficient with** time-management, and completing tasks when they are assigned to me.

* 'advantage'를 활용한 문장은 다음과 같이 수정해야 한다:
= My time-management skills gives me an **advantage** over others, when assigned with tasks.

2) <... and completing tasks when they are assigned to me>는 분사구문으로서 이것을 부사절로 바꾸면 다음과 같다: <... and I complete tasks when they are assigned to me>

**** 보충설명**: 장점을 뜻하는 어휘의 다양한 활용

My **strength** is **in** time-management and multi-tasking.
I **excel in** my research skills.
I am **proficient in** MS Word and MS Excel.
I am **efficient in** basic accounting and bookkeeping.
The **assets** that I can bring into the company are my resourcefulness and ambition.
Research and writing are my **strong points**.
= My **strong points** are research and writing.
The **advantage** I have over other candidates is my work experience with the government department when I worked there as an intern.
The **merit** of being a member of a large team is that it allows you to collaborate with people who have different opinions from yours, and you can learn from others' expertise.

4. So I do most of the work on time without delay.
(그래서 저는 대부분의 일들을 지체없이 제 시간에 해냅니다.)
<on time / without delay>
→ I do most of the work on time**,** without delay.

**** 원어민 설명**

<time> 뒤에 쉼표(,)를 붙이는 것이 더 적합한 표현이라고 한다. 이에 대한 원어민의 생각을 들어보자:
I can't explain why I put the comma there, but it does belong there. Please see below. My examples might explain it better than I can. The sentence can be written like this:

① I do most of the work on time.
② I do most of the work without delay.
③ I do most of the work on time and without delay.
④ I do most of the work on time, without delay.

5. To be honest, I chose chinese because I had to go on to college.
(솔직히 말하면 제가 중국어를 선택한 이유는 대학에 진학하기 위해서였습니다.)
<to be honest / go on to college>
→ To be honest, I chose **Chinese** because I had to go on to college.
= To be honest, I chose **Chinese** because I had to **go to** college.

6. I didn't have anything I wanted to do at the time.
(그 당시 저는 하고 싶었던 것이 아무 것도 없었습니다.)
<at the time>
→ I **did not** have anything I wanted to do at the time.

7. when I was in second grade in the high school, I chose to take a second foreign language class.
(고등학교 2학년 때, (저는) 제2외국어 수업을 받기로 선택했습니다.)

<second foreign language / take a class>

→ **When** I was in **the** second grade **in high school,** I chose to take a second foreign language class. (△)

→ When I was **a second-year student in high school,** I chose to take a second foreign language class. (△)

** **보충설명**: 북미 학제에 따른 학년 표시

위에서 수정한 두 문장이 문법적으로 적합한 문장임에도 불구하고 끝에 세모 표시로 기재한 이유는 실제로 북미에서 이런 표현을 사용하지 않는다는 점 때문이다. 미국과 캐나다에서는 각 지역에 따라 다른 학제를 채택하고 있는데, 예를 들어 캐나다 대부분의 주에서 사용하고 있는 5-3-4 학제 (Elementary school 5년 - Middle school 3년 - High school 4년)에서의 고등학교 2학년 학생과 우리나라의 경우처럼 6-3-3 학제를 사용하는 주에서의 고등학교 2학년 학생은 실제 학년이 다르기 때문에 <the second grade in high school>이라는 표현은 혼돈을 줄 수 있다. 따라서 이러한 혼돈을 줄이기 위해 5-3-4 학제이든 6-3-3 학제이든 심지어는 7-5학제 (밴쿠버의 경우는 Elementary 7년+중고등학교를 합해 High school 5년으로 운용)에서도 이러한 의무교육 기간을 다 합치면 12년이기 때문에 grade 1~ grade 12라는 표현을 사용한다. 결국 우리나라 고등학교 2학년 학생에 해당하는 경우에는 5-3-4학제에서든 6-3-3학제에서든 grade 11을 사용하여 다음과 같이 표현하는 것이 적절하다:

→ When I was **in grade 11**, I chose to take a second foreign language class. (O)

** 참고: 미국에서는 다음과 같은 표현도 가능하다:

When I was **a sophomore in high school**, I chose to take a second foreign language class.
= When I was **a high school sophomore**, I chose to take a second foreign language class.

8. Later, I became interested in Chinese after my mother recommended a Chinese language academy.
(얼마 후, 어머니께서 중국어학원을 추천해 주신 후에 (저는) 중국어에 관심을 가지게 되었습니다.)

<Chinese language academy>

→ **correct**

** **대체 가능한 표현들**:

① Later, **my interest in Chinese grew** after my mother (had) recommended a Chinese language academy.

② Later, I **was** interested in Chinese after my mother recommended a Chinese language academy. (O)

③ Later, I **became** interested in Chinese after my mother recommended a Chinese language academy. (OO)

* 동사 'was' 대신에 '**became**'을 사용할 때 보다 확실한 의미를 나타낸다.

≠ Later, I got interested in Chinese after my mother recommended a Chinese language academy.

* 'got interested'는 구어체 표현으로서 공식문서용으로 적합하지 않다.

9. So I chose an university department related to China.
(그래서 저는 중국과 관련된 대학 학과를 선택했습니다.)

→ **As a result**, I chose **a** university department related to China.

= **Therefore,** I chose **a** university department related to China.

* 공식적인 문서에서 'so' 대신, 'as a result' 혹은 'therefore'를 쓰는 것이 좋다.

10. Last year, I went to Taiwan with my friend.
(작년에, 저는 친구와 함께 대만에 갔습니다.)

→ **correct**

11. My friend wasn't good at Chinese, so I was almost in charge of Chinese.
(제 친구는 중국어를 잘하지 못해서 제가 거의 중국어를 담당했습니다.)

<good at / in charge of>

* 일반적으로 <be good at>은 <~에 능숙한>의 뜻이다. 그러나 <be good at>은 비격식체 표현이기 때문에 공식문서에서는 <be proficient in> 혹은 <be proficient with>로 바꾸어 표현하는 것이 바람직하다:

→ My friend **was not proficient in/with the language**, so I was **almost always** in charge of **communicating** in Chinese.

* 위 문맥에서 <almost (거의)>를 <almost always (대부분)>로 수정해야 올바른 문장이 된다. 또한 '담당한 것'이 중국어가 아니라 '중국어로 소통한 것'이기 때문에 <in charge of communicating in Chinese> 가 되어야 한다

12. As I was in contact with Chinese at restaurants and tourist attractions, It was not easy to speak Chinese, but it was fun to talk in Chinese.
(제가 식당과 관광명소에서 중국인과 만났을 때, 중국어로 말하는 것이 쉽지 않았지만 중국어로 이야기하는 것은 재미있었습니다.)

<in contact with / tourist attractions>

→ When I was in contact with **the Chinese people** at restaurants and tourist attractions, **it** was not easy to speak Chinese, but it was **fun.**

= When I was in contact with **the people** at restaurants and tourist attractions, **it** was not easy to speak Chinese, but it was **fun.**

= When I was in contact with **the Chinese-speaking people** at restaurants and tourist attractions, **it** was not easy to speak Chinese, but it was **fun.**

= When I **interacted** with the Chinese people at restaurants and tourist attractions, it was not easy to speak Chinese, but it was fun.

**** 원어민 설명**

원어민 시각에서 본 바람직한 문장은 다음과 같다:

This included speaking and interacting with the people at restaurants and tourist attractions. It was not easy to speak Chinese, but it was fun.

**** 보충설명: 잘못 영작된 사례**

① When I was in contact with the Chinese people at restaurants and tourist attractions, it was not easy to speak Chinese but fun. **(X)**

② When I was in touch with the Chinese people at restaurants and tourist attractions, it was not easy to speak Chinese but it was fun. **(X)**

**** 참고: <in contact with>와 <in touch with>의 차이점**

<in contact with>와 <in touch with>는 둘 다 <~와 접촉하다> 혹은 <~와 연락하다>라는, 거의 동일한 의미를 지닌 관용적 표현이다. 두 구문(phrase)의 미묘한 뉘앙스의 차이를 살펴보면, 전자의 경우 상대방과 직접 만나거나 정기적으로 반복해서 전화나 메일로 소통하는 상황을 뜻한다면, 후자의 경우에는 먼 거리에 있는 상대방과 전화를 하거나 메일을 보냄으로써 소통을 하는 것을 말한다. 따라서 상대방과 직접 만나는 위의 상황에서는 <in touch with>가 아니라 <in contact with>가 되어야 맞는 표현이다.

13. And when I was in my first year of college, I joined an international exchange network.
(그리고 대학교 1학년 때, (저는) 국제교류모임에 가입했습니다.)

→ **correct**

**** 대체 가능한 표현**

① When I was **in the first year at college/university,** I joined an international exchange network.

② When I was **a first-year student at college,** I joined an international exchange network.

③ When I was **a freshman in college,** I joined an international exchange network.

14. I felt it was fun to talk and interact with foreign friends.
(외국인 친구들과 대화하고 교류하는 것은 즐겁다고 생각했습니다.)

→ **correct**

* 위 문장을 좀 더 명확하게 표현하기 위해서는 다음과 같은 문장도 가능하다:

I felt it was fun to talk **to** and interact with foreign friends.

15. So I would like to have a job related to Chinese language.
(그래서 저는 중국어와 관련된 직장을 얻고 싶습니다.)

→ **As a result,** I would like to have a job related to **the** Chinese language.
= **Therefore,** I would like to have a job related to **the** Chinese language.
≠ **Therefore,** I would like to have a job related to **Chinese**. **(X)**

**** 원어민 설명**

위의 세 번째 문장이 틀린 이유에 대한 원어민의 설명이다:

I would use the first and second sentence. The third sentence is ambiguous because when you say "related to Chinese" it can also refer to the "Chinese people", since in the previous sentences, not only were you discussing the Chinese language, but interacting with the people, as well. It is unclear in the third sentence if you are referring to Chinese.

Part 5 Final Draft

Hello, my name is Kim, Namyeob, and my major is Chinese. I **grew up under** my parents, who did not **put** much **pressure on** me to study. I am **proficient in** time-management, and completing tasks when they are assigned to me. I do most of the work **on time, without delay. To be honest**, I chose Chinese because I had to **go on to college**. I did not have anything I wanted to do **at the time**. When I was in grade 11, I chose to **take a** second foreign language **class**. Later, my interest in Chinese grew after my mother recommended a Chinese language academy. **As a result**, I chose a university department **related to** China. Last year, I went to Taiwan with my friend. My friend was not **proficient in** the language, so I was almost always **in charge of** communicating in Chinese. This[3)] included speaking and interacting with people at restaurants and tourist attractions. It was not easy to speak Chinese, but it was fun. When I was in my first year of college, I joined an international exchange network. I felt it was fun to talk to and interact with foreign friends. Therefore, I would like to have a job **related to** the Chinese language.

3) <this> refers to her being the one who was communicating in Chinese.

Fundamental Exercises

1. 다음 문장을 올바르게 수정하시오.

<hi my name is kim hyo mi my major is chinese.>

→ ____

2. 다음 문장을 읽고 밑줄 친 부분에 들어갈 적합한 구(phrase)를 고르시오.

I ____________________ I wanted to do at the time.

① didn't have something
② did not has something
③ did not have anything
④ didn't has anything

3. 다음 문장을 읽고 빈 칸에 적합한 전치사를 적으시오.

I am proficient _________ time-management, and completing tasks when they are assigned to me.

4. 다음 문장을 읽고 이를 격식체 문체로 바꾸어 다시 쓰시오.

So I chose a university department related to China.

→ ____

5. 다음 문장을 읽고 틀린 부분을 수정하여 전체 문장을 다시 쓰시오.

When I was in touch with the Chinese people at restaurants and tourist attractions, it was not easy to speak Chinese, but fun.

→ ____

____

Personal statement

Mary Grace Hwang

Growth Background

"A proud only child of a family"

I was born as an only child to my parents who work for securities companies. Back in my childhood, I grew up learning the importance of effort and responsibility from my parents. My mother and father, who have tried to raise me the right person, always told me "Success is proportional to effort." Grown up with them, I have lived as a person who works hard for my job to the end, and there was full support from my parents. I had a cheerful and healthy schooldays not to disappoint them, and I also learned courage from them.

Personality

"A driven leader"

Positive drive and leadership are the strongest points of my character. With my personality like this, I have been a 'trustworthy person' among my friends. Knowing that I can seem too authoritative, I'm always trying to be more thoughtful, and to get my growth in human relationships, and understanding more people's situations.

"Work responsibly"

My motto is "Doing it right the first time, of course with the responsibility." I used to be told that I was too meticulous because of my character, but I was able to experience a lot of representative experience thanks to my personality.

College Experience

In 2018, I entered the Department of Americas Trade and Culture at Hyupsung University, and have been getting into the spirit of my college life. I have worked as a student class representative and a member of the student council of the College of Business Administration since I was in my sophomore year, with an interest in promoting the students' rights and great college life. I struggled to listen to every student's opinion and felt rewarded for making a better campus.

Furthermore, I received scholarships for 4 years in university and worked in a student college promotion team in 2021. I also have 3 awards in various in-university contests.

Career Goals

In the digital-economy era, online and offline borders are gradually disappearing. In various regions, different types of companies are competing to satisfy their consumer who has higher expectations. We have to quickly understand consumer's wants with changing trends. I want to be a future-oriented person who will lead the company with active drive, not just a passive employee.

I really appreciate your reading. I certify that the above information is all true.

Part 7 해석

자기소개서

황 메리 그레이스

성장배경

"자랑스러운 외동 딸"

저는 증권사에서 일하시는 부모님 사이에서 외동으로 태어났습니다. 어린 시절, 저는 부모님으로부터 노력과 책임감의 중요성에 대해 배우며 자랐습니다. 저를 바른 사람으로 키우기 위해 노력하신 어머니와 아버지께서는 항상 저에게 "성공은 노력에 비례한다"고 말씀하셨습니다. 부모님과 함께 성장을 하면서, 저는 제가 맡은 일을 끝까지 열심히 해내는 사람으로 살고 있으며 부모님으로부터의 전적인 지원이 있었습니다. 저는 부모님을 실망시켜 드리지 않도록 밝고 건전한 학창 시절을 보냈으며, 부모님으로부터 용기 또한 배웠습니다.

성격

"의욕이 넘치는 리더 "

긍정적인 추진력과 리더십은 제 성격의 가장 큰 강점입니다. 이와 같은 성격을 지닌 저는 친구들 사이에서 '신뢰할 수 있는 사람' 이 되었습니다. 너무 권위적으로 보일 수 있다는 것을 알기에, 저는 인간관계에서 항상 더 사려 깊고, 성숙하려고 하며, 더 많은 사람들의 입장을 이해하려고 노력하고 있습니다.

"책임감 있게 일하는 사람"

제 좌우명은 "처음부터 제대로 해라, 물론 책임감 있게"입니다. 저는 성격 때문에 지나치게 꼼꼼하다는 말을 듣곤 했지만, 제 성격 덕분에 많은 리더 경험을 하기도 했습니다.

대학 경험

2018년, 저는 협성대학교 미주통상문화학과에 입학하여 열정적인 대학생활을 해 왔습니다. 저는 학생들의 권익을 증진시키는 것과 멋진 대학 생활을 하는 것에 관심을 가지고 2학년부터 과대표 및 경영대학 학생회의 일원으로 활동하였습니다. 저는 모든 학생들의 의견을 경청하기 위해 노력했으며 더 나은 캠퍼스를 만드는데 보람을 느꼈습니다.

뿐만 아니라, 저는 4년간 교내 장학금을 받았으며 2021년에는 학교 홍보단원으로 활동하였습니다. 또한, 다양한 교내 공모전에서 수상을 3번 했습니다.

포부(목표)

디지털 경제 시대에 온라인과 오프라인 상의 경계는 점점 사라지고 있습니다. 여러 지역에서 다양한 업종의 회사들이 더 높은 기대를 가진 소비자들을 만족시키기 위해 경쟁하고 있습니다. 우리는 변화하는 트랜드와 함께 소비자들이 원하는 것을 신속하게 파악해야 합니다. 저는 단순히 수동적인 사원이 아니라, 능동적인 추진력을 가지고 기업을 이끌어 나갈 미래지향적인 인재가 되고 싶습니다.

읽어주셔서 대단히 감사합니다. 상기 내용은 모두 사실임을 확인합니다

<English Words and Idioms>

securities companies 증권사 (참고: securites 증권)
responsibility 책임감
proportional 비례하는
full support 전적인 지원
to the end 끝까지, 마지막까지
cheerful 밝은
schooldays 학창시절

personality 성격
driven 의욕이 넘치는
drive 추진력
trustworthy 신뢰할 수 있는, 믿을 수 있는
authoritative 권위적인
thoughtful 사려 깊은
situation 입장
motto 좌우명
do it right the first time 처음부터 제대로 해라
used to ~ 하곤 했다 (과거의 불규칙적인 습관) (참고: be used to ~ing ~하는데 익숙하다)
meticulous 꼼꼼한
character 성격
characteristic 사람마다 가지고 있는 고유한 특성

thanks to ~덕분에

enter 입학하다
Department of Americas International Trade and Culture 미주통상문화학과
get into the spirit of ~에 열정적으로 참여하다
student class representative 과대표
student council 학생회
College of Business Administration 경영대학
sophomore 2학년 (참고: freshman : 1학년, junior : 3학년, senior : 4학년)
promote ~을 증진시키다, ~을 촉진시키다
great 멋진
college life 대학생활
struggle 역경을 견디며 어렵게 해내다
feel rewarded for ~에 대해 보람을 느끼다
scholarship 장학금
in-university 교내의

digital-economy era 디지털 경제시대
border 경계
gradually 점차
disappear 사라지다 = be done away
compete 경쟁하다
future-oriented 미래지향적인
active 능동적인
just 단순히, 단지
passive 수동적인
appreciate 감사하다, 인정하다, 높이 평가하다
certify 확인하다, 증명하다

Part 8 영작연습

다음 문장을 올바르게 수정하시오

자기소개서

Personal statement

→ ____________________

성장배경

Growth Background

→ ____________________

"자랑스러운 외동 딸"

"A proud only child of a family"

→ ____________________

저는 증권사에서 일하시는 부모님 사이에서 외동으로 태어났습니다.

I was born as an only child to my parents who work for securities companies.

→ ____________________

어린 시절, 저는 부모님으로부터 노력과 책임감의 중요성에 대해 배우며 자랐습니다.

Back in my childhood, I grew up learning the importance of effort and responsibility from my parents.

→ ____________________

____

저를 바른 사람으로 키우기 위해 노력하신 어머니와 아버지께서는 항상 저에게 "성공은 노력에 비례한다"고 말씀하셨습니다.

My mother and father, who have tried to raise me the right person, always told me "Success is proportional to effort."

→ ____

____

부모님과 함께 성장을 하면서, 저는 제가 맡은 일을 끝까지 열심히 해내는 사람으로 살고 있으며 부모님으로부터의 전적인 지원이 있었습니다.

Grown up with them, I have lived as a person who works hard for my job to the end, and there was full support from my parents.

→ ____

____

저는 부모님을 실망시켜 드리지 않도록 밝고 건전한 학창 시절을 보냈으며, 부모님으로부터 용기 또한 배웠습니다.

I had a cheerful and healthy schooldays not to disappoint them, and I also learned courage from them.

→ ____

____

성격

Personality

→ ____________

" 의욕이 넘치는 리더 "

"A driven leader"

→ ________________

긍정적인 추진력과 리더십은 제 성격의 가장 큰 강점입니다.

Positive drive and leadership are the strongest points of my character.

→ ____

이와 같은 성격을 지닌 저는 친구들 사이에서 '신뢰할 수 있는 사람'이 되었습니다..

With my personality like this, I have been a 'trustworthy person' among my friends.

→ ____________________

____

너무 권위적으로 보일 수 있다는 것을 알기에, 저는 인간 관계에서 항상 더 사려 깊고, 성숙하려고 하며, 더 많은 사람들의 입장을 이해하려고 노력하고 있습니다.

Knowing that I can seem too authoritative, I'm always trying to be more thoughtful, and to get my growth in human relationships, and understanding more people's situations.

→ ____________________

____

____

"책임감 있게 일하는 사람"

"Work responsibly"

→ ____________________

제 좌우명은 "처음부터 제대로 해라, 물론 책임감 있게"입니다.

My motto is "Doing it right the first time, of course with the responsibility."

→ ____________________

저는 성격 때문에 지나치게 꼼꼼하다는 말을 듣곤 했지만, 제 성격 덕분에 많은 리더 경험을 하기도 했습니다.

I used to be told that I was too meticulous because of my character, but I was able to experience a lot of representative experience thanks to my personality.

→ ____________________

____

대학 경험

College Experience

→ ____________________

2018년, 저는 협성대학교 미주통상문화학과에 입학하여 열정적인 대학생활을 해 왔습니다.

In 2018, I entered the Department of Americas Trade and Culture at Hyupsung University, and have been getting into the spirit of my college life.

→ ____

____

저는 학생들의 권익을 증진시키는 것과 멋진 대학 생활을 하는 것에 관심을 가지고 2학년부터 과대표 및 경영대학 학생회의 일원으로 활동하였습니다.

I have worked as a student class representative and a member of the student council of the College of Business Administration since I was in my sophomore year, with an interest in promoting the students' rights and great college life.

→ ____

____

____

저는 모든 학생들의 의견을 경청하기 위해 노력했으며 더 나은 캠퍼스를 만드는 데 보람을 느꼈습니다.

I struggled to listen to every student's opinion and felt rewarded for making a better campus.

→ ____

____

뿐만 아니라, 저는 4년간 교내 장학금을 받았으며 2021년에는 학교 홍보단원으로 활동하였습니다.

Furthermore, I received scholarships for 4 years in university and worked in a student college promotion team in 2021.

→ ____

____

또한 다양한 교내 공모전에서 수상을 3번 했습니다.

I also have 3 awards in various in-university contests.

→ ______________________________

포부(목표)

Career Goals

→ __________

디지털 경제 시대에 온라인과 오프라인 상의 경계는 점점 사라지고 있습니다.

In the digital-economy era, online and offline borders are gradually disappearing.

→ ______________________________

여러 지역에서, 다양한 업종의 회사들이 더 높은 기대를 가진 소비자들을 만족시키기 위해 경쟁하고 있습니다.

In various regions, different types of companies are competing to satisfy their consumer who has higher expectations.

→ ______________________________

____

우리는 변화하는 트랜드와 함께 소비자들이 원하는 것을 신속하게 파악해야 합니다.

We have to quickly understand consumer's wants with changing trends.

→ ______________________________

저는 단순히 수동적인 사원이 아니라, 능동적인 추진력을 가지고 기업을 이끌어 나갈 미래 지향적인 인재가 되고 싶습니다.

I want to be a future-oriented person who will lead the company with active drive, not just a passive employee.

→ ______________________________

____

읽어주셔서 대단히 감사합니다.

I really appreciate your reading.

→ ______________________________

상기 내용은 모두 사실임을 확인합니다.

I certify that the above information is all true.

→ ____

Part 9 정답과 해설

자기소개서

Personal statement

→ **Cover Letter**

= Letter of Self-Introduction

성장배경

Growth Background

→ **Background**

= Personal Background

"자랑스러운 외동 딸"

"A proud only child of a family"

→ **An only child of the** family **who is proud of her**

**** 원어민 설명**

'A proud only child of a family' is an odd phrase to say. But 'An only child of the family who is proud of her' might be better. The reason I say that this sentence is odd (no matter how it is edited) is because it is usually not needed for someone to say that their family is proud of their child.

저는 증권사에서 일하시는 부모님 사이에서 외동으로 태어났습니다.

I was born as an only child to my parents who work for securities companies.

→ **correct**

어린 시절, 저는 부모님으로부터 노력과 책임감의 중요성에 대해 배우며 자랐습니다.

Back in my childhood, I grew up learning the importance of effort and responsibility from my parents.

→ **I grew up learning about** the importance of effort and responsibility from my parents.

저를 바른 사람으로 키우기 위해 노력하신 어머니와 아버지께서는 항상 저에게 "성공은 노력에 비례한다"고 말씀하셨습니다.

My mother and father, who have tried to raise me the right person, always told me "Success is proportional to effort."

→ My mother and father, who have tried to raise me **as a good person**, always told me "Success is proportional to effort."

→ **I was taught that** "Success is proportional to effort."

부모님과 함께 성장을 하면서, 저는 제가 맡은 일을 끝까지 열심히 해내는 사람으로 살고 있으며 부모님으로부터의 전적인 지원이 있었습니다.

Grown up with them, I have lived as a person who works hard for my job to the end, and there was full support from my parents.

→ **Growning up with this**, I have lived as a person who works hard for my job to the end.

* 부모님과 함께 성장을 한 것보다, 부모님의 가르침(성공은 노력에 비례한다)과 더불어 성장한 결과 현재의 내가 될 수 있었다는 것에 초점을 두어야 한다.

저는 부모님을 실망시켜 드리지 않도록 밝고 건전한 학창 시절을 보냈으며, 부모님으로부터 용기 또한 배웠습니다.

I had a cheerful and healthy schooldays not to disappoint them, and I also learned courage from them.

* 복수명사(schooldays) 앞에 관사(a)가 올 수 없다.

→ I had cheerful and **sound** schooldays **in order** not to disappoint **my family, from whom** I also learned courage.

* to부정사의 부사적 역할, 다시 말해 <목적>의 의미를 명확하게 기재할 필요가 있기 때문에 <not to disappoint>를 <in order not to disappoint>로 수정하는 것이 좋다.

= I had cheerful and **sound** schooldays **in order** not to disappoint my family. **I also learned courage from them**.

= I had cheerful and **sound** schooldays **in order** not to disappoint my family. **They also taught me courage**.

**** 보충설명**

이 문맥에서 다시 살펴보아야 할 것은 우리나라와 다른 영미권 국가의 문화이다. 예를 들어 우리나라에서는 학생 개인이 부모님의 기대에 부흥하기 위해 밝고 건전한 학창시절을 보낼 수 있지만, 영미권 국가에서는 개인이 고등학교를 졸업하고 나면 부모님으로부터 벗어나 독립적인 생활을 시작하기 때문에 이런 식의 사고방식, 즉 부모님의 기대를 충족시키기 위해 밝고 건전한 학창시절을 보낸다는 것은 영미권 문화적 배경에서는 적절하지 않은 내용이다.

성격

Personality

→ **correct**

" 의욕이 넘치는 리더 "

"A driven leader"

→ **OK**
→ "**Purpose-driven leader**" (better)

긍정적인 추진력과 리더십은 제 성격의 가장 큰 강점입니다.
Positive drive and leadership are the strongest points of my character.
→ **correct**

이와 같은 성격을 지닌 저는 친구들 사이에서 '신뢰할 수 있는 사람'이 되었습니다..
With my personality like this, I have been a 'trustworthy person' among my friends.
→ **With this personality**, I have been a 'trustworthy person' among my friends.
= **I am known to be** a trustworthy person among my friends.

너무 권위적으로 보일 수 있다는 것을 알기에, 저는 인간 관계에서 항상 더 사려 깊고, 성숙하려고 하며, 더 많은 사람들의 입장을 이해하려고 노력하고 있습니다.
Knowing that I can seem too authoritative, I'm always trying to be more thoughtful, and to get my growth in human relationships, and understanding more people's situations.
→ **grammatically incorrect**

* 'relationship'은 인간관계를 의미하기 때문에 앞에 'human'을 붙일 필요가 없다

→ Knowing that I **could** seem too authoritative, I am always trying to be more thoughtful, **to grow and expand my relationships,** and **to understand other** people's situations.

* **병렬구조**(parallel structure): to be / to grow and expand / to understand

→ **Because I know** that I could seem too authoritative, I am always trying to be more thoughtful, **to grow and expand my relationships,** and **to understand other** people's situations.

"책임감 있게 일하는 사람"
"Work responsibly"
→ **correct**

제 좌우명은 "처음부터 제대로 해라, 물론 책임감 있게"입니다.
My motto is "Doing it right the first time, of course with the responsibility."
→ My motto is "**Do** it right the first **time with** the responsibility."

저는 성격 때문에 지나치게 꼼꼼하다는 말을 듣곤 했지만, 제 성격 덕분에 많은 리더 경험을 하기도 했습니다.
I used to be told that I was too meticulous because of my character, but I was able to experience a lot of representative experience thanks to my personality.

* 위 문장에서 학생이 언급한 성격, 다시 말해 '지나치게 꼼꼼한 성격'과 '리더 경험'과의 연관성이 없기 때문에 전체 문장을 다시 바꾸어야 할 필요가 있다. 이때 우선적으로 알아두어야 할 것은 personality와 character 그리고 characteristic의 차이이다.

** **보충설명**: **personality, character, characteristic** 차이

personality: 밖으로 쉽게 드러나는 성격 – shy, friendly, outgoing → 예문: Elise has a complex personality. She is quiet in class, but when she is with her friends she is loud and confident.
character: 오랜 시간 상대방을 보아야 알 수 있는 인품이나 인성 – honest, trustworthy, → 예문: Elise is warm-hearted. She welcomes everyone with a smile.
characteristic: 상대방을 드러내는 특성 → 예문: You can always tell when Elise has entered the room, because you can hear her quiet voice and laughter.

⬇

따라서 위의 문장을 수정하면 다음과 같다:

→ I used to be told that I was too meticulous, but **that characteristic helped me to focus.**
= I used to be told that I was too meticulous, but **that characteristic gave me focus.**

대학 경험
College Experience
→ **correct**

2018년, 저는 협성대학교 미주통상문화학과에 입학하여 열정적인 대학생활을 해 왔습니다.
In 2018, I entered the Department of Americas Trade and Culture at Hyupsung University, and have been getting into the spirit of my college life.
→ In 2018, I entered the Department of Americas **International** Trade and Culture at Hyupsung University, and have been getting into the spirit of my college life.

저는 학생들의 권익을 증진시키는 것과 멋진 대학 생활을 하는 것에 관심을 가지고 2학년부터 과대표 및 경영대학 학생회의 일원으로 활동하였습니다.
I have worked as a student class representative and a member of the student council of the College of Business Administration since I was in my sophomore year, with an interest in promoting the students' rights and great college life.
→ I have worked as a student class representative and a member of the student council of the College of Business Administration since I was in my sophomore year, with an interest in promoting the students' rights and **having a** great college life.
* 병렬구조: promoting / having

저는 모든 학생들의 의견을 경청하기 위해 노력했으며 더 나은 캠퍼스를 만드는 데 보람을 느꼈습니다.

I struggled to listen to every student's opinion and felt rewarded for making a better campus.
→ I **endeavoured** to listen to every student's opinion and felt rewarded for making a better campus.

** **보충설명**: '**struggle**'과 '**endeavour**'의 차이

struggle: 역경을 견디며 어렵게 해내다 ('to try very hard to do, with difficulty') **endeavour:** 목표를 이루기 위해 노력하다/ 굳은 의지를 가지고 노력하다 ('to strive to achieve or reach', or 'serious determined effort,') **examples:** I struggled to complete my Math homework before it was due. I endeavoured to complete my Math homework before the bell rang.

뿐만 아니라, 저는 4년간 교내 장학금을 받았으며 2021년에는 학교 홍보단원으로 활동하였습니다.

Furthermore, I received scholarships for 4 years in university and worked in a student college promotion team in 2021.

* 학교 홍보단원은 <campus ambassador>와 <student representative>로 표기할 수 있다.

→ **As a result of my hard work,** I **awarded** scholarships for 4 years in university and worked **as a campus ambassador** in 2021.
= **As a result of my hard work,** I **awarded** scholarships for 4 years in university and worked **as a student representative** in 2021.
= **As a result of my hard work,** I **awarded** scholarships for 4 years in university and **helped with student recruitment** in 2021.
* 장학금 수혜여부와 관련하여, <receive>보다 <award>가 자기소개서에 더 적합한 격식체 표현이다

또한 다양한 교내 공모전에서 수상을 3번 했습니다.

I also have 3 awards in various in-university contests.

* 시제가 '과거'이기 때문에 과거동사를 사용해야 한다. 이때 기억해야 할 것은 <~을 수상하다>에 해당하는 가장 적합한 동사가 <win>, <award>, <earn>이고, 그 외에도 <receive>를 사용할 수도 있다는 점이다. 그러나 이 문맥에서 <have>나 <gain>동사를 쓰면 공식문서에 적합하지 않은 문장으로 간주된다.

→ I also **won** 3 awards in various in-university contests. (OO)
= I also **awarded** 3 awards in various in-university contests. (OO)
= I also **earned** 3 awards in various in-university contests. (OO)

→ I also **received** 3 awards in various in-university contests. (O)
≠ I also **had** 3 awards in various in-university contests. (Δ)
≠ I also **gained** 3 awards in various in-university contests. (Δ)

포부(목표)

Career Goals

→ OK

→ **Goals** or **Objectives** (O)

** **원어민 설명**: If this is for a heading, it can just say "Goals" or "Objectives"

디지털 경제 시대에 온라인과 오프라인 상의 경계는 점점 사라지고 있습니다.

In the digital-economy era, online and offline borders are gradually disappearing.

→ **correct**

= In the digital-economy era, online and offline borders **are** gradually **done away**.

여러 지역에서, 다양한 업종의 회사들이 더 높은 기대를 가진 소비자들을 만족시키기 위해 경쟁하고 있습니다.

In various regions, different types of companies are competing to satisfy their consumer who has higher expectations.

→ In various regions, different types of companies are competing to satisfy their **consumers** who **have** higher expectations.

우리는 변화하는 트랜드와 함께 소비자들이 원하는 것을 신속하게 파악해야 합니다.

We have to quickly understand consumer's wants with changing trends.

→ We have to quickly understand **consumers'** wants with changing trends.

= We **need** to quickly understand **consumers'** wants with changing trends.

저는 단순히 수동적인 사원이 아니라, 능동적인 추진력을 가지고 기업을 이끌어 나갈 미래지향적인 인재가 되고 싶습니다.

I want to be a future-oriented person who will lead the company with active drive, not just a passive employee.

→ **just gramatically correct** (△)

* 이 문장은 문법적으로 올바르지만 내용과 관련해서 수정해야 할 필요가 있다. 왜냐하면 지원자의 목표가 미래지향적인 인재가 되는 것이 아니라 미래지향적인 인재로서 '지원하고자 하는 회사를 이끌어 가고자하는 자신의 의지'를 나타내야 하기 때문이다. 따라서 다음과 같이 수정하는 것이 좋다:

① **As a future-oriented person, I wish to help lead the company with active drive, and not as a passive employee.**

② **I hope to grow with the company, and take an active role in helping the company succeed.**

③ **As a future-oriented person, I look forward to growing with the company and playing an active role in the company's success.**

읽어주셔서 대단히 감사합니다.

I really appreciate your reading.

* 동명사(reading)의 목적어인 <this letter>가 누락되어 있다.

→ I really appreciate your reading **this letter**.

= I really appreciate **your interest**.

상기 내용은 모두 사실임을 확인합니다.

I certify that the above information is all true.

→ **not necessary**

* 이 내용은 법률 문서(legal document)에 해당하는 표현으로서 자기소개서 내용으로 적합하지 않다.

Fundamental Exercises

1. 다음 문장을 읽고 틀린 부분을 수정하여 전체 문장을 다시 쓰시오.

Knowing that I could seem too authoritative, I am always trying to be more thoughtful, to grow and expand my relationships, and understanding other people's situations.

→ ______________________________

____

____

2. 다음 문장을 읽고 밑줄 친 단어의 뜻을 선택하시오.

Positive <u>drive</u> and leadership are the strongest points of my character.

① 동력 ② 운전실력 ③ 추진력 ④ 충동

3. 다음 문장을 읽고 틀린 부분을 수정하여 전체 문장을 다시 쓰시오.

I struggled to listen to every student's opinion and felt rewarded about making a better campus.

→ ______________________________

____

4. 다음 문장을 읽고 밑줄 친 구문(phrase)의 정확한 뜻을 고르시오.

I was known to be a trustworthy person <u>among my friends</u>.

① 두 명의 친구들
② 두 명이 채 안 되는 친구들
③ 세 명 이하의 친구들
④ 세 명 이상의 친구들

5. 다음 문장을 읽고 빈 칸에 들어갈 올바른 구문을 고르시오.

I had cheerful and sound schooldays ______________ disappoint my family, from whom I also learned courage. (저는 가족을 실망시키지 않도록 밝고 건전한 학창 시절을 보냈으며, 가족으로부터 또한 용기를 배웠습니다.)

① in order to not ② as so not to ③ in order not to ④ not to so as

Part 10 Instructor's First Revision

Cover Letter

Background

'An only child of the family who is proud of her'

I was born as an only child to my parents who work for securities companies. I grew up learning about the importance of effort and responsibility from my parents. My mother and father, who have tried to raise me as a good person, always told me "Success is proportional to effort." Growning up with this, I have lived as a person who works hard for my job to the end. I had cheerful and sound schooldays in order not to disappoint my family, from whom I also learned courage.

Personality

'A purpose-driven leader'

Positive drive and leadership are the strongest points of my character. With this personality, I have been a 'trustworthy person' among my friends. Knowing that I could seem too authoritative, I am always trying to be more thoughtful, to grow and expand my relationships, and to understand other people's situations.

"Work responsibly"

My motto is "Do it right the first time with the responsibility." I used to be told that I was too meticulous, but that characteristic helps me to focus.

College Experience

In 2018, I entered the Department of Americas International Trade and Culture at Hyupsung University, and have been getting into the spirit of my college life. I have worked as a student class representative and a member of the student council of the College of Business Administration since I was in my sophomore year, with an interest in promoting the students' rights and having a great college life. I endeavoured to listen to every student's opinion and felt rewarded for making a better campus.
As a result of my hard work, I awarded scholarships for 4 years in university and worked as a campus ambassador in 2021. I also won 3 awards in various in-university contests.

Goals

In the digital-economy era, online and offline borders are gradually disappearing. In various regions, different types of companies are competing to satisfy their consumers who have higher expectations. We have to quickly understand consumers' wants with changing trends. As a future-oriented person, I wish to help lead the company with active drive, and not as a passive employee.

I really appreciate your reading this letter.

Part 11 Instructor's Second Revision Based on the Cover Letter Format

Cover Letter

Sender's name
and address

Contact information (phone number, email, any website address or other social media, etc)

Date

To Whom It May Concern:

My name is ________________, a recent graduate at Hyupsung University, who is ready to embark on a career of ________________. I feel <name of company> would benefit from my knowledge, skills, and drive for success. I grew up learning about the importance of effort and responsibility from my parents. I was taught that "Success is proportional to effort." Growing up with this, I have lived as a person who works hard for my job to the end. In the digital-economy era, online and offline borders are gradually disappearing. In various regions, different types of companies are competing to satisfy their customers, who have higher expectations. We have to quickly understand consumers' wants with changing trends. I believe I am the right person to do this.

Positive drive and leadership are the strongest points of my character. In 2018, I entered the Department of Americas International Trade and Culture at Hyupsung University, and have gotten into the spirit of my college life. I have worked as a student class representative and a member of the student council of the College of Business Administration since I was in my sophomore year, with an interest in promoting the students' rights and having a great college life. I am always trying to be thoughtful and to grow in my understanding of others. I endeavoured to listen to every student's opinion, and felt rewarded for making a better campus.

My motto is "Do it right the first time, with responsibility." I used to be told that I was too meticulous, but that characteristic helped me to focus. As a result of my hard work, I awarded scholarships for 4 years in university, and worked as a campus ambassador in 2021. I also won 3 awards in various in-university contests.

I am looking for a company that will appreciate my talents, and that will help me to grow continuously in the ______ profession. I want to be a future-oriented person who will lead the company with active drive, not just a passive employee. I really appreciate your reading this letter, and I will gladly meet with you to discuss any future employment at <name of company>.

Sincerely,

Sender's Name

Part 12 Translation into Korean for the Instructor's Second Revision

지원자(발신자) 이름

주소

연락처 (전화번호, 이메일 주소, 기타 웹사이트 주소/소셜 미디어 연락처 정보 등)

발신 날짜

인사말

저는 협성대학교를 최근에 졸업하고 _________ 분야의 직업을 구하려고 하는 ________입니다. 저는 제가 가지고 있는 지식과 기술, 그리고 성공을 향한 추진력이 <지원한 회사명>에 도움이 될 것이라고 생각합니다. 저는 부모님으로부터 노력과 책임감의 중요성에 대해 배우며 성장했습니다. (저는) "성공은 노력에 비례한다"는 가르침을 받았습니다. 이러한 가르침과 더불어 성장을 하면서, 저는 제가 맡은 일을 끝까지 열심히 하는 사람으로 살아왔습니다. 디지털 경제시대에서 온라인과 오프라인의 경계가 점차 사라지고 있습니다. 여러 지역에서, 다양한 업종의 회사들이 더 높은 기대를 가진 소비자들을 만족시키기 위해 경쟁하고 있습니다. 우리는 변화하는 트랜드와 함께 소비자들이 원하는 것을 신속하게 파악해야 합니다. 저는 이것을 할 수 있는 적임자라고 생각합니다.

긍정적인 추진력과 리더십은 제 성격의 가장 큰 강점입니다. 저는 2018년 협성대학교 미주통상문화학과에 입학하여 열정적인 대학생활을 해 오고 있습니다. 저는 학생들의 권익을 증진시키는 것과 멋진 대학 생활을 하는 것에 관심을 가지고 2학년 때부터 과대표 및 경영대학 학생회의 일원으로 활동하였습니다. 저는 사려 깊고 타인에 대한 이해를 넓혀가기 위해 항상 노력하고 있습니다. 저는 모든 학생들의 의견을 경청하려고 노력하였으며, 더 나은 캠퍼스를 만드는 것에 대해 보람을 느꼈습니다.

제 좌우명은 "책임감을 가지고 처음부터 똑바로 하자"입니다. 한 때 제가 지나치게 꼼꼼하다는 말을 듣긴 했지만, 그 성격은 제가 집중을 하도록 도와주었습니다. 열심히 공부한 결과, 저는 4년 동안 장학금을 받았으며, 2021년에는 학교 홍보단원으로 활동하였습니다. 또한, 저는 다양한 교내 공모전에서 수상을 3번 했습니다.

저는 저의 재능을 높이 인정하고 ________ 직종에서 제가 지속적으로 성장할 수 있도록 도움을 줄 회사를 찾고 있습니다. 저는 단순히 수동적인 사원이 아니라, 능동적인 추진력을 가지고 회사를 이끌어 나갈 미래지향적인 인재가 되고 싶습니다. 읽어주셔서 대단히 감사드리며, 향후 <응모한 회사명>의 채용에 대해 논의하게 된다면 기쁜 마음으로 선생님을 만나 뵙겠습니다.

끝인사,

발신자 이름

<English Words and Idioms>

concern 관련하다
To Whom It May Concern 관계자에게 (담당자 귀하)
recent graduate 최근 졸업생
embark on ~에 착수하다, ~을 시작하다.
　embark 승선, 탑승, 적재, (새 사업 등의) 착수
career 직업
benefit from ~로부터 이익을 얻다, ~로부터 도움을 받다
drive for ~을 향한 추진력
proportional to ~에 비례하는
border 경계
convey 알리다, 전하다
grow 발전시키다(develop)
characteristic 사람마다 가지고 있는 고유한 특성
　character 성격
endeavour 목표를 이루기 위해 노력하다/ 굳은 의지를 가지고 노력하다
work 공부하다, 활동하다
as a result of ~의 결과로서
　'as a result' 결과적으로, 그래서
profession (전문적인) 직업, 직종
meet with ~와 만나다

Part 13 영작연습

다음 문장을 영작하시오.

자기소개서

→ ____________________

지원자 이름 및 주소

(예: 황 메리 그레이스

22192 대한민국 인천시 미추홀구 매소홀로 68, 501동 1301호)

→ ____________________

____

____

연락처

(예: sunflower@hanmail.net)

010 – 1234 - 5678

→ ____________________

____

발신 날짜

→ ____________________

담당자 귀하

→ ____________________

1. The First Paragraph

저는 협성대학교를 최근에 졸업하고 마케팅 분야의 직업을 구하려고 하는 황 메리 그레이스 입니다.

→ ______________________________

____

<my name / recent graduate / ready to embark on / career of>

저는 제가 가지고 있는 지식과 기술, 그리고 성공을 향한 추진력이 <지원한 회사명>에 도움이 될 것이라고 생각합니다.

→ ______________________________

____

<feel / name of company benefit from / drive for>

저는 부모님으로부터 노력과 책임감의 중요성에 대해 배우며 성장했습니다.

→ ______________________________

<grow up / learning about>

저는 "성공은 노력에 비례한다"는 가르침을 받았습니다.

→ ______________________________

<be taught / proportional to>

이러한 가르침과 더불어 성장을 하면서, 저는 제가 맡은 일을 끝까지 열심히 하는 사람으로 살아왔습니다.

→ ______________________________

____

<growing up / as / who / my job / to the end>

디지털 경제시대에서 온라인과 오프라인의 경계가 점차 사라지고 있습니다.

→

<digital-economy era / borders / disappear>

여러 지역에서, 다양한 업종의 회사들이 더 높은 기대를 가진 소비자들을 만족시키기 위해 경쟁하고 있습니다.

→

<various / different types of / compete / consumers / expectations>

우리는 변화하는 트랜드와 함께 소비자들이 원하는 것을 신속하게 파악해야 합니다.

→

<have to / understand / changing trends>

저는 이것을 할 수 있는 적임자라고 생각합니다.

→

<right person to>

2. The Second Paragraph

긍정적인 추진력과 리더십은 제 성격의 가장 큰 강점입니다.

→ ______________________________

<positive drive / character>

저는 2018년 협성대학교 미주통상문화학과에 입학하여 열정적인 대학생활을 해 오고 있습니다.

→ ______________________________

____

<enter / Department of Amercas International Trade and Culture / get into the spirit of ~ >

저는 학생들의 권익을 증진시키는 것과 멋진 대학 생활을 하는 것에 관심을 가지고 2학년 때부터 과대표 및 경영대학 학생회의 일원으로 활동하였습니다.

→ ______________________________

____

<student class representative / student council / College of Business Administration / in my sophomore year / with an interest in promoting ... and having>

저는 사려 깊고 타인에 대한 이해를 넓혀가기 위해 항상 노력하고 있습니다.

→ ______________________________

<trying to / thoughtful / grow in / others>

저는 모든 학생들의 의견을 경청하려고 노력하였으며, 더 나은 캠퍼스를 만드는 것에 대해 보람을 느꼈습니다.

→ ______________________________

____

<endeavour / opinion / feel rewarded for>

3. The Third Paragraph

제 좌우명은 "책임감을 가지고 처음부터 똑바로 하자"입니다.

→ ______________________________

<motto / do it right the first time>

한 때, 제가 지나치게 꼼꼼하다는 말을 듣긴 했지만, 그 성격은 제가 집중을 하도록 도와주었습니다.

→ ______________________________

____

<used to / meticulous / characteristic>

열심히 공부한 결과, 저는 4년 동안 장학금을 받았으며, 2021년에는 학교 홍보단원으로 활동하였습니다.

→ ______________________________

____

<as a result of my hard work / work / campus ambassador>

또한, 저는 다양한 교내 공모전에서 수상을 3번 했습니다.

→ ______________________________

<win / in-university contests>

4. The Fourth Paragraph

저는 저의 재능을 높이 인정하고, 마케팅 직종에서 제가 지속적으로 성장할 수 있도록 도움을 줄 회사를 찾고 있습니다.

→ ______________________________

____

<look for / appreciate / help me to grow / profession>

저는 단순히 수동적인 사원이 아니라, 능동적인 추진력을 가지고 회사를 이끌어 나갈 미래 지향적인 인재가 되고 싶습니다.

→ ______________________________

____

<want / future-oriented person / lead / active drive / passive employee>

읽어주셔서 대단히 감사드리며, 향후 <응모한 회사명>의 채용에 대해 논의하게 된다면 기쁜 마음으로 선생님을 만나 뵙겠습니다.

→ ______________________________

____

<appreciate ~ing / meet with / to discuss / any future employment>

끝인사,

→ ______________

지원자 이름

→ ______________

Part 14 정답과 해설

자기소개서

→ Cover Letter

지원자 이름 및 주소

(예: 황 메리 그레이스

22192 대한민국 인천시 미추홀구 매소홀로 68, 501동 1301호)

→ Mary Grace Hwang = Hwang, Mary Grace
501-1301, 68, Maesohol-ro, Michuhol-gu, Incheon, 22192
Repulic of Korea

연락처

(예: sunflower@hanmail.net)

010 – 1234 - 5678

→ sunflower@hanmail.net
+82-10-1234-5678

발신 날짜

(예: 2022년 9월 30일)

→ September 30, 2022

담당자 귀하

→ To Whom It May Concern:

1. The First Paragraph

저는 협성대학교를 최근에 졸업하고 마케팅 분야의 직업을 구하려고 하는 황 메리 그레이스입니다.

<my name / recent graduate / ready to embark on / career of>

→ My name is Mary Grace Hwang, a recent graduate at (from) Hyupsung University, who is ready to embark on a career of marketing.

저는 제가 가지고 있는 지식과 기술, 그리고 성공을 향한 추진력이 <지원한 회사명>에 도움이 될 것이라고 생각합니다.

<feel / name of the company benefit from / drive for>

→ I **feel** <name of company> **will benefit from** my knowledge, skills, and drive for success.

* 이 문맥에서 동사 <think>도 가능하지만 지원자의 강인한 의지를 내포하는 <feel>이나 <believe>가 더 적합하다.

→ I **believe** <name of company> **will beneffit from** my knowledge, skills, and drive for success.
= I believe my knowledge, skills, and drive for success **will help** <name of company>.

저는 부모님으로부터 노력과 책임감의 중요성에 대해 배우며 성장했습니다.
<grow up / learning about>

→ I grew up learning about the importance of effort and responsibility from my parents.

저는 "성공은 노력에 비례한다"는 가르침을 받았습니다.
<be taught / proportional to>

→ I was taught that "Success is proportional to effort."

이러한 가르침과 더불어 성장을 하면서, 저는 제가 맡은 일을 끝까지 열심히 하는 사람으로 살아왔습니다.
<growing up / as / who / my job / to the end>

→ **Growing up** with this, I have lived as a person who works hard for my job to the end.
= **Having grown up** with this, I have lived as a person who works hard for my job to the end.

디지털 경제시대에서 온라인과 오프라인의 경계가 점차 사라지고 있습니다.
<digital-economy era / borders / disappear>

→ In the digital-economy era, online and offline borders are gradually disappearing
= In the digital-economy era, online and offline borders are gradually **done away.**

여러 지역에서, 다양한 업종의 회사들이 더 높은 기대를 가진 소비자들을 만족시키기 위해 경쟁하고 있습니다.
<various / different types of / compete / consumers / expectations>

→ In various regions, different types of companies are competing to satisfy their customers, who have higher expectations.

우리는 변화하는 트랜드와 함께 소비자들이 원하는 것을 신속하게 파악해야 합니다.
<have to / understand / changing trends>

→ We have to quickly understand consumers' wants with changing trends.

저는 이것을 할 수 있는 적임자라고 생각합니다.
<right person to>

→ I **feel** I am the right person to do this.
= I **believe** I am the right person to do this.

* 이 문맥에서 동사 <think>도 가능하지만 지원자의 강인한 의지를 내포하는 <feel>이나 <believe>가 더 적합하다.

2. The Second Paragraph

긍정적인 추진력과 리더십은 제 성격의 가장 큰 강점입니다.
<positive drive / character>

→ Positive drive and leadership are the strongest points of my character.

저는 2018년 협성대학교 미주통상문화학과에 입학하여 열정적인 대학생활을 해 오고 있습니다.
<enter / Department of Amercas International Trade and Culture / get into the spirit of ~ >

→ In 2018, I entered the Department of Americas International Trade and Culture at Hyupsung University, and **have gotten into the spirit of my college life.**

= In 2018, I entered the Department of Americas International Trade and Culture at Hyupsung University, and **have been getting into the spirit of my college life.**

저는 학생들의 권익을 증진시키는 것과 멋진 대학 생활을 하는 것에 관심을 가지고 2학년 때부터 과대표 및 경영대학 학생회의 일원으로 활동하였습니다.
<student class representative / student council / College of Business Administration / in my sophomore year / with an interest in promoting ... and having>

→ I **have worked** as a student class representative and a member of the student council of the College of Business Administration **since** I was in my sophomore year, with an interest in promoting the students' rights and having a great college life.

저는 사려 깊고 타인에 대한 이해를 넓혀가기 위해 항상 노력하고 있습니다.
<trying to / thoughtful / grow in / others>

→ I **am** always **trying** to be thoughtful and to grow in my understanding of others.

= I **have** always **tried** to be thoughtful and to grow in my understanding of others.

* 원어민 설명: 위 문맥에서 동명사의 의미상의 주어 <my>를 생략하면 틀린 문장이 된다.

저는 모든 학생들의 의견을 경청하려고 노력하였으며, 더 나은 캠퍼스를 만드는 것에 대해 보람을 느꼈습니다.
<endeavour / opinion / feel rewarded for>

→ I endeavoured to listen to every student's opinion, and felt rewarded for making a better campus.

3. The Third Paragraph

제 좌우명은 "책임감을 가지고 처음부터 똑바로 하자"입니다.
<motto / do it right the first time>

→ My motto is "Do it right the first time, with responsibility."

한 때, 제가 지나치게 꼼꼼하다는 말을 듣긴 했지만, 그 성격(특성)은 제가 집중을 하도록 도와주었습니다.

<used to / meticulous / characteristic>

→ I **used to be told** that I was too meticulous, but that characteristic helped me to focus.
= I **was told** that I was too meticulous, but that characteristic helped me to focus.
≠ I used to ~~listen~~ that I was too meticulous, but that characteristic helped me to focus. (X)

* 북미사람들의 경우에는 help 뒤에 목적격 보어로 원형부정사보다 to부정사를 더 선호한다.

열심히 공부한 결과, 저는 4년 동안 장학금을 받았으며, 2021년에는 학교 홍보단원으로 활동하였습니다.

<as a result of my hard work / work / campus ambassador>

* <장학금을 받다>에 해당하는 가장 적합한 동사로 <win>과 <award>를 들 수 있고, 그 외에 가능한 동사로 <receive>를 활용할 수도 있다. 그러나 <have>나 <gain> 동사를 쓰면 공식문서에 적합하지 않은 문장이 된다.

→ As a result of my hard work, I **won** scholarships for 4 years in (at) university, and worked as a campus ambassador in 2021. (OO)
= As a result of my hard work, I **awarded** scholarships for 4 years in (at) university, and worked as a campus ambassador in 2021. (OO)

→ As a result of my hard work, I **received** scholarships for 4 years in (at) university, and worked as a campus ambassador in 2021. (O)

≠ As a result of my hard work, I **had** scholarships for 4 years in (at) university, and worked as a campus ambassador in 2021. (△)
≠ As a result of my hard work, I **gained** scholarships for 4 years in (at) university, and worked as a campus ambassador in 2021. (△)

**** 대체 가능한 표현들:**

As a result of my hard work, I awarded scholarships for 4 years **while I was in(at) university,** and worked as a campus ambassador in 2021.
= As a result of my hard work, I awarded scholarships for 4 years **while in(at) university,** and worked as a campus ambassador in 2021.

또한, 저는 다양한 교내 공모전에서 수상을 3번 했습니다.

<win / in-university contests>

* <~을 수상하다>에 해당하는 가장 적합한 동사로는 <win>, <award>, <earn>을 들 수 있고, 그 외에도 <receive>를 사용할 수도 있다. 그러나 <have>나 <gain>동사를 쓰면 공식문서에 적합하지 않은 문장으로 간주된다.

→ I also **won** 3 awards in various in-university contests. (OO)
= I also **awarded** 3 awards in various in-university contests. (OO)
= I also **earned** 3 awards in various in-university contests. (OO)

→ I also **received** 3 awards in various in-university contests. (O)

≠ I also **had** 3 awards in various in-university contests. (Δ)
≠ I also **gained** 3 awards in various in-university contests. (Δ)

4. The Fourth Paragraph

저는 저의 재능을 높이 인정하고, 마케팅 직종에서 제가 지속적으로 성장할 수 있도록 도움을 줄 회사를 찾고 있습니다.

<look for / appreciate / help me to grow / profession>

→ I am looking for a company that **will** appreciate my talents, and **that will help** me (to) grow continuously in the marketing profession. (OO)

* 이 문장에서 will은 화자의 적극적인 의지를 반영한다 **(more active)**

= I am looking for a company that **will** appreciate my talents, and **help** me (to) grow continuously in the marketing profession.

* 'company' 앞에 'a'가 아니라 'the'를 붙이면 틀린 문장이 된다.
* 'the marketing profession' 앞에 'at'를 붙이면 틀린 문장이 된다.

= I am looking for a company that **would** appreciate my talents, and that **would** help me (to) grow continuously in the marketing profession. (O)

* 이 문장에서 would는 화자의 소극적인 의향을 반영한다 **(more passive)**
* 이 문맥에서 관계대명사 <which>를 사용하면 틀린 문장이 된다.

**** 원어민 설명:**

문법적으로 보았을 때 위 문장에서 우리가 사용할 수 있는 관계대명사로는 <that>과 <which> 둘 다 가능하지만, 이와 달리 북미 현지에서는 <which>가 아니라 <that>만 사용된다고 한다.

저는 단순히 수동적인 사원이 아니라, 능동적인 추진력을 가지고 회사를 이끌어 나갈 미래지향적인 인재가 되고 싶습니다.

<want / future-oriented person / lead / active drive / passive employee>

→ I want to be a future-oriented person who will lead the company with active drive, not just a passive employee.

읽어주셔서 대단히 감사드리며, 향후 <응모한 회사명>의 채용에 대해 논의하게 된다면 기쁜 마음으로 선생님을 만나 뵙겠습니다.
<appreciate ~ing / meet with / to discuss / any future employment>

> **** 원어민 설명:**
>
> <~ meet with you ~> 대신에 <~ meet you ~>를 써도 가능한 표현이지만 원어민의 시각으로 더 바람직한 것은 <~ meet with you ~>라고 한다.

→ I really appreciate your reading this letter, and I **will** gladly meet with you **to discuss** any future employment at <name of company>. - **직설법 조건문: 단순가정 (00)**

= I really appreciate your reading this letter, and I **would** gladly meet with you **to discuss** any future employment at <name of company>. - **가정법 과거 (0)**

끝인사,

→ Sincerely,

지원자 이름

→ Mary Grace Hwang

Part 15 Final Draft

Cover Letter

Mary Grace Hwang
501-1301, 68, Maesohol-ro, Michuhol-gu
Incheon, 22192
Repulic of Korea

sunflower@hanmail.net
+82-10-1234-5678

September 30, 2022

To Whom It May Concern:

My name is Mary Grace Hwang, a recent graduate at Hyupsung University, who is ready to embark on a career of marketing. I feel <name of company> will benefit from my knowledge, skills, and drive for success. I grew up learning about the importance of effort and responsibility from my parents. I was taught that "Success is proportional to effort." Growing up with this, I have lived as a person who works hard for my job to the end. In the digital-economy era, online and offline borders are gradually disappearing. In various regions, different types of companies are competing to satisfy their customers, who have higher expectations. We have to quickly understand consumers' wants with changing trends. I believe I am the right person to do this.

Positive drive and leadership are the strongest points of my character. In 2018, I entered the Department of Americas International Trade and Culture at Hyupsung University, and have gotten into the spirit of my college life. I have worked as a student class representative and a member of the student council of the College of Business Administration since I was in my sophomore year, with an interest in promoting the students' rights and having a great college life. I am always trying to be thoughtful and to grow in my understanding of others. I endeavoured to listen to every student's opinion, and felt rewarded for making a better campus.

My motto is "Do it right the first time, with responsibility." I used to be told that I was too meticulous, but that characteristic helped me to focus. As a result of my hard work, I awarded scholarships for 4 years in university, and worked as a campus ambassador in 2021. I also won 3 awards in various in-university contests.

I am looking for a company that will appreciate my talents, and that will help me to grow continuously in the marketing profession. I want to be a future-oriented person who will lead the company with active drive, not just a passive employee. I really appreciate your reading this letter, and I will gladly meet with you to discuss any future employment at <name of company>.

Sincerely,

Mary Grace Hwang

Mary Grace Hwang

Enclosure: resume

Fundamental Exercises

1. 다음 문장을 올바르게 수정하여 전체 문장을 다시 쓰시오.

My motto is "Doing it right the first time, with responsibility".

→ ______________________________

2. 다음 내용을 읽고 이에 적합한 영어문장을 고르시오.

한때 제가 지나치게 꼼꼼하다는 말을 듣긴 했지만, 그 성격은 제가 집중을 하도록 도와주었습니다.

① I was used to be told that I was too meticulous, but that personality helped me to focuses.
② I used to listen that I was very meticulous, but that characteristic helped me to focus.
③ I used to be told that I was too meticulous, but that characteristic helped me to focus.
④ I was used to listening that I was too meticulous, but that character helped me to focus.

3. 다음 문장에서 밑줄 친 부분에 들어갈 적합하지 않은 동사를 고르시오.

I also ________ 3 awards in various in-university contests.

① awarded ② won ③ had ④ earned

4. 다음 문장을 읽고 밑줄 친 to부정사의 의미를 고르시오.

I really appreciate your reading this letter, and I will gladly meet with you to discuss any future employment at <name of company>.

① 원인 ② 목적 ③ 결과 ④ 조건

5. 다음 문장을 읽고 밑줄 친 부분에 적합한 관계대명사를 적으시오.

I am looking for a company ________ will appreciate my talents, and ________ will help me to grow continuously in the marketing profession.

→ ______________________________

3장

영문 자기소개서

우리나라나 북미 기업에서 신입사원 채용과정에서의 공통적인 사항이라 할 수 있는 것은 취업준비생들이 회사에 지원할 때 주로 온라인으로 자기소개서와 이력서를 접수하고, 인사담당자가 지원자들의 자기소개서와 이력서를 검토한 후 후보자들을 선별하여 개별적으로 연락한다는 것이다. 한 가지 차이라고 볼 수 있는 것은, 한국회사들은 대부분 지원자들의 자기소개서와 이력서를 함께 제출할 것을 요구하지만, 이와 달리 북미에 있는 회사들은 경우에 따라 자기소개서를 필수적인 제출 조건으로 삼지 않는다는 점이다. 이러한 이유에서 북미 회사에 지원을 하는 경우, 그 회사의 채용규정을 면밀히 살펴본 후 자기소개서의 제출여부를 결정해야 한다. 그러나 일반적으로 북미에서 수용되고 있는 표준적인 채용과정에서는 자기소개서와 이력서 둘 다 제출하는 것을 기준으로 한다. 다음은 북미기업에서의 일반적인 채용절차이다.

Step 1:

Apply for the job by doing the following (depending on the company's requirements). It is very important to read the instructions carefully.

a) Fill out an online application form on their website. The website will also indicate if a cover letter or resume is required.
b) Submit a cover letter and resume to an email address, or submit it through their website.
c) Submit a resume only, plus filling out an application form online.

Step 2:

The employer will read through all the applications, and will create a short-list.... a list of candidates that they are interested in interviewing. At this point, you may never hear from the employer because they did not select you for the short-list.

Step 3:

If the employer is interested in interviewing you, they will contact you, usually by telephone, and sometimes by email, to arrange for the interview.

Step 4:

Attend the interview. Dress appropriately for the interview, usually in business-casual clothes. At the interview, there may be more than one person interviewing you. Bring a hard-copy of your resume, in case extra copies are needed. Also, bring your "references" to the interview – one sheet of paper that has at least 3 "references" that the employer can contact, regarding your work history and qualifications. This can include anyone that you've worked with, or worked for in the past, anyone whom you volunteered with or volunteered for, and personal references / friends who are **not family members**. Personal references can be friends with whom you have a good relationship. At the end of the interview, you can offer to provide a list of references, if you remembered to bring it, or if the employer asks for it.

Step 5:

In some cases, there may be a second interview with either the same interviewers, or with additional interviewers. If a second interview is required, the employer will inform you of the hiring process during the first interview.

Step 6:

After the interview, you can follow-up with a thank-you email, or thank you card, thanking them for interviewing you.

Step 7:

If the employer decides to hire you, they will contact you again. Depending on the employer, they might also call you to inform you that they have hired someone else.

Hiring steps and processes can vary depending on the size of the company. Some small companies will have a more easy and basic method for hiring (1 interview only). Larger companies can have several steps. Additional steps might also include a police-record check, to ensure you have not been convicted of a crime. Other companies will do a credit check on your finance, to check if you have bad credit... Banks and other financial companies might have this requirement. Some small companies will have a verbal agreement, and say "we would like to hire you" and arrangements would be made on the phone. Other employers will email a letter of offer, detailing the start-date and pay-rate of the position.

*** A note on references[4]:**

Always ask the person before adding them to your reference list, in case they are not comfortable being contacted by an employer. For example, a teacher that teaches 300 students may not be the best reference to ask, unless you have an exceptional relationship with the teacher. If you were the type of student who sat at the back of the class, and did not interact with the teacher, then it may not be a good idea to ask the teacher to be a reference.

4) <reference>는 지원자에 대해 참고할 수 있는 정보, 예를 들어 지원자의 실력, 업무태도, 성격 등에 대해 피드백을 줄 수 있는 인물로서 추천인을 의미한다. 추천인을 선택할 때 지원자의 성향이나 실력에 대해 잘 파악하고 있는 멘토나 직장 상사를 선정하는 것이 좋다. 지원자가 경력자인 경우 자신이 근무했던 직장의 직속상사나 직장 동료 등의 연락처를 기재하면 되고, 졸업예정자인 경우에는 지도교수나 같은 학교 출신의 친구나 선배 등의 연락처를 쓰면 된다. 지원자의 역량이나 자질에 대해 보증할 수 있는 제3자를 의미하기 때문에 친인척의 경우는 이에 해당되지 않는다.

Sample reference page:

Header:
Your name
Your address
Your city, state, and postal code
Your phone number
Your email address

References

Bob Gordon	(name of reference)
Principal, ABC School	(title and place of work)
Waterloo ON	(city and province)
111-987-6543	(phone number)
bob.gordon@email.ca	(his/her email address)

Joanna Lee
Marketing Director, Lee Agency
Kitchener ON
666-111-2345
lee.joanna@email.ca

Roanna Rodriguez
Honours Project Partner, ABC School
Waterloo ON
111-515-1515
rodriguezr@email.ca

Part 1 Cover Letter

Cover Letter(영문 자기소개서)는 취업준비생이 입사 지원할 때 편지형식으로 작성하여 이력서와 더불어 제출하는 공식문서를 말한다. 기본 취지는 인사담당자에게 자신을 소개하는 것이지만 해당 포지션 및 업무에 자신이 가장 적합한 인재라는 것을 부각시켜야 하는 목적이 훨씬 크다. 대부분의 인사담당자들은 커버레터를 이력서만큼 중요하게 간주하지 않는 경향을 보이기도 하지만, 담당자에 따라 이를 꼼꼼하게 읽은 후 지원자의 이력서를 읽을지에 대한 여부를 결정하기 때문에 보다 세밀하게 신경을 써서 작성해야 할 필요가 있다. 그 과정에서 이력서에 기재된 스펙위주의 내용을 중복해서 쓰기보다는 이력서에서 표현하지 않았던 내용들, 예를 들어 지원동기라든지 업무에 대한 관심 그리고 남들과 차별화된 자신만의 경험과 역량을 구체적으로 드러내고, 앞으로 이를 더욱 확장시켜 회사에 기여하겠다는 목표의식을 부각시켜야 한다. 앞에서 언급한 것처럼, 커버레터는 이력서 내용을 보완해주는 편지형태의 문서이기 때문에 이력서보다는 덜 딱딱하면서도 간결하게 자신의 업무수행 능력에 대해 쓰는 것이 포인트이다. 국문 자기소개서와 달리 영문 자기소개서에서는 자신의 단점이라든지 사생활, 예를 들어 가족이나 종교, 성적 취향 등에 대해서는 절대 언급하지 말아야 한다. 이에 대한 원어민의 시각은 다음과 같다:

> Main difference between Asia and Canada with cover letters or letters of introduction is that we try not to discuss our families or personal life. It is focused on qualifications, skills, education and work experiences. Any "personal" information can be mentioned in the interview, and even then, it should not be brought up by the employer, since it is illegal to discriminate on sexual orientation, religion, family, etc.. Examples... you cannot be denied a job because of who you are married to, your gender, if you have children, if your parents are divorced, if you are vegetarian etc.. Therefore, the employer should not ask about that as part of the hiring process. If, however, the interviewee (you) mention it during a job interview, then that is ok. They just cannot use that information in their decision to hire you. Having said all that, it does not mean that employers do not discriminate, but by avoiding some of those topics of conversation, it lessens the ability of the employer to use that information to discriminate.

커버레터는 편지인 동시에 이력서의 표지역할을 하기 때문에 한 페이지가 넘어가지 않는 짧은 분량으로 4~5 문단으로 간단하게 작성한다. 채용 담당자는 커버레터를 통해 지원자의 업무능력과 영어 문서작성 능력을 동시에 보기 때문에 지원자는 자신의 영어표현이 적절했는지 확인해야 할 뿐만 아니라 올바른 문법과 적절한 어휘를 사용했는지에 대해서도 다시 세심하게 살펴야 한다.

영문 비즈니스문서의 기본 양식으로는 총 6가지, 구체적으로 Semi-Block Form, Block Form, Full-Block Form, Indented Form, Hanging Indented Form, Simplified Form이 있다. 이러한 양식 중에서 어떤 것을 선택할 지는 개인의 몫이지만 근래에 업무용으로 주로 사용되고 있는 대표 서식으로는 Block Form을 들 수 있다. 경우에 따라 Indented Form이 사용되기도 한다. 이 두 양식 모두 행간은 single space, 즉 행간 여백이 없는 기본정렬이다.

1. Block Form

비즈니스 문서에서 가장 대표적인 양식으로서 모든 단락의 시작을 왼쪽으로 정렬한다.

Example:

Mary Grace Hwang
265 Park Street
Akron OH, 12345
marygrace@hanmail.net
area code – 123-1234

Recruiter's Name
Campus Recruiter
Company Name
Company Address

February 20, 2021

Dear Campus Recruiter:

I am a senior at Massachusetts Business College majoring in marketing with a communications minor. I am very impressed with MC Agency's approach to advertising and promotion as presented by Amy Wright. MC Agency's ability to form diverse strategies to tackle all the problems a client may have is impressive. I believe in blending innovative marketing strategies with more traditional methods, especially when it comes to online media. My approach to marketing will always be client-focused, and results-based. With this in mind, I am writing to request an invitation to interview for a Marketing Assistant position with MC Agency.

In the past two years, I worked as a volunteer for Urban Animal Rescue, a none-profit company that rescues and rehabilitates small urban wildlife. As their marketing consultant, I helped to evaluate and implement marketing strategies to educate the public about the rescue's mission. Through TikTok, Instagram, and Youtube, the marketing team was able to aim the rescue's educational campaign to a younger audience. I spent a lot of time working with the content team to improve engagement from social media posts, blogs, and newsletters.

My communications minor is an asset to my work and education in marketing. It has allowed me to embrace and appreciate new media's impact on the public psyche. Every platform has its base audience, and by understanding not only the media itself, but it's audience has helped me to become better and more effective with my approach to advertising. Together, with my knowledge and passion in marketing, I have yielded results in unexpected ways through analysis and creative problem-solving.

I am very excited about the opportunity to work with MC Agency, and I welcome the opportunity to speak with you about the ways in which I can contribute to the company. Thank you and I look forward to hearing from you soon.

Sincerely,

Mary Grace Hwang

Mary Grace Hwang

Enclosure: resume

2. Indented Form

서론, 본론, 결론에 해당하는 문단을 시작할 때 들여쓰기를 하는 양식으로서 일반적으로 날짜, 끝인사 그리고 서명은 가운데(중앙) 정렬을 한다.

Example:

Mary Grace Hwang
265 Park Street
Akron OH, 12345
marygrace@hanmail.net
area code- 123-1234

February 20, 2021.

Recruiter's Name
Campus Recruiter
Company Name
Company Address

Dear Campus Recruiter:

I am a senior at Massachusetts Business College majoring in marketing with a communications minor. I am very impressed with MC Agency's approach to advertising and promotion as presented by Amy Wright. MC Agency's ability to form diverse strategies to tackle all the problems a client may have is impressive. I believe in blending innovative marketing strategies with more traditional methods, especially when it comes to online media. My approach to marketing will always be client-focused, and results-based. With this in mind, I am writing to request an invitation to interview for a Marketing Assistant position with MC Agency.

In the past two years, I worked as a volunteer for Urban Animal Rescue, a none-profit company that rescues and rehabilitates small urban wildlife. As their marketing consultant,

I helped to evaluate and implement marketing strategies to educate the public about the rescue's mission. Through TikTok, Instagram, and Youtube, the marketing team was able to aim the rescue's educational campaign to a younger audience. I spent a lot of time working with the content team to improve engagement from social media posts, blogs, and newsletters.

My communications minor is an asset to my work and education in marketing. It has allowed me to embrace and appreciate new media's impact on the public psyche. Every platform has its base audience, and by understanding not only the media itself, but it's audience has helped me to become better and more effective with my approach to advertising. Together, with my knowledge and passion in marketing, I have yielded results in unexpected ways through analysis and creative problem-solving.

I am very excited about the opportunity to work with MC Agency, and I welcome the opportunity to speak with you about the ways in which I can contribute to the company. Thank you and I look forward to hearing from you soon.

Sincerely,

Mary Grace Hwang
Mary Grace Hwang

Enclosure: resume

Part 3 General Outline of a Cover Letter

Header (발신자 정보)

Receiver's information (수신자 정보- 이름 및 소속회사명/주소 등) **- OPTIONAL**
(This is necessary if you are sending the cover letter by mail or paper, but it is not necessary if you are emailing the cover letter.)

Date (발신 날짜)

Salutation (인사말)

Introduction paragraph (서론)

Body paragraphs (본론)

Concluding paragraph (결론)

Closing (끝인사)

Signature and your name (자필서명과 지원자 이름)

Part 4 How to write a Cover Letter

I. Header: 발신자(지원자) 이름과 연락처를 적는 난

This should include your name and contact information, including address, phone number, and email. If you have other contact information, such as a website, then you can include that here, as well.

**** 참고:**

header는 경우에 따라 어느 정도 독창적으로 작성할 수 있다. 예를 들어 글자크기를 키운다든지, 글의 모양을 바꾸거나 왼쪽 정렬이 아닌 다른 정렬로 변경할 수도 있고, 나아가 글자를 컬러로 입힐 수도 있다. 그러나 너무 요란하지 않은 무난한 색상과 적당한 글자 사이즈를 선택함으로써 일반적인 자기소개서 양식에서 크게 벗어나지 않는 것이 좋다.

1. First Name Last Name (발신자 이름)

→ 이름은 full name으로 <이름 성> 혹은 <성, 이름>의 순서로 쓴다.

(Ex) Namyeob Hwang
Hwang, Namyeob

2. Sender's Address (발신자 주소) - (번지, 동, 구, 시, 우편번호, 국가 – 국제우편인 경우)

→ 영어권 국가의 주소표기 방식은 우리나라의 방식과 반대되는 순서로 쓴다.

Street address **City** **State/ Province** **Postal code** **Country**

(Ex) 미국주소

11939 S Normal Ave Chicago IL, 60628 USA

(Ex) 한국 도로명주소 (아파트): 22192 대한민국 인천시 미추홀구 매소홀로 68, 501동 1301호

501-1301, 68, Maesohol-ro, Michuhol-gu, Incheon, 22192, Republic of Korea ⬇ 501-1301, 68, Maesohol-ro, Michuhol-gu Incheon, 22192 Republic of Korea

→ 일반 시(city)의 경우 –si를 지역명 뒤에 붙여야 하지만 <서울특별시>와 <광역시>의 경우에는 –si를 붙이지 않아도 된다.

→ 대한민국 정식 영문명은 <Republic of Korea>이고, 통상적으로는 <South Korea>가 자주 사용된다.

(Ex) 한국 도로명주소 (주택): 02609 대한민국 서울시 동대문구 답십리로 210

210, Dapsimni-ro, Dongdaemun-gu, Seoul, 02609, Korea ⬇ 210, Dapsimni-ro, Dongdaemun-gu Seoul, 02609 Korea

→ Korea의 경우 'Republic of Korea' 또는 'South Korea'로 명시함으로써 북한이 아님을 분명히 한다. 단 주소지가 서울인 경우에는 'Korea'라고 표기해도 무방하다.

(Ex) 한국 지번주소 (아파트): 22192 대한민국 인천시 남구 용현5동 금호2차 아파트 501-1301

501-1301, Kumho 2 Cha Apt., Yonghyeon 5-dong, Nam-gu, Incheon, 22192, Republic of Korea ⬇ 501-1301, Kumho 2 Cha Apt. Yonghyeon 5-dong, Nam-gu Incheon, 22192 Republic of Korea

(Ex) 한국 지번주소 (주택): 02873 대한민국 서울시 성북구 보문동 7가 100번지

100, Bomundong-7st, Seongbuk-gu, Seoul, 02873, Korea ⬇ 100, Bomundong-7st, Seongbuk-gu Seoul, 02873 Korea

3. Sender's Phone Number (발신자 전화번호)

① 국내 거주자가 해외기업에 지원하는 경우

a) 유선전화(일반전화):

→ + 한국국가번호(country code) - 지역번호(area code) - 전화번호(phone #)

각 나라마다 (우리나라의 001, 002 혹은 00700과 같은) 국제전화인식번호가 있다. 따라서 해외에서 우리나라로 국제전화를 거는 경우, 지원자가 국제전화인식번호에 해당하는 번호를 지정해서 기입하는 것이 아니라 전화를 거는 상대방, 즉 인사담당자가 자신이 거주하는 나라의 국제전화인식번호를 선택해서 전화를 해야 한다. 따라서 국가번호 앞에 +를 붙인 것은 상대방이 국제전화인식번호를 선택하여 전화를 걸도록 표시한 것이다.

유선전화번호를 적는 과정에서 유의해야 할 것은 지역번호에서 앞자리 숫자 <0>을 제외하고 기재해야 한다는 점이다. 예를 들어 서울과 인천의 지역번호가 <02>와 <032>인데 국제전화의 경우에는 앞의 숫자 0을 빼고 각각 <2>와 <32>만 적으면 된다.

(Ex) 서울의 경우: +82 – 2 – * * * – * * * *
(Ex) 인천의 경우: +82 – 32 – * * * – * * * *

b) 무선전화(휴대전화):

→ + 한국국가번호 – 휴대폰번호

무선전화인 경우에는 지역번호 없이 국가번호 뒤에 바로 휴대폰번호만 기재한다, 이 경우에도 유의해야 할 것은 휴대폰번호에서 앞자리 숫자 <0>은 제외하고 기재해야 한다는 점이다.

(Ex) +82 – 10 – * * * * – * * * *

② 해외 거주자가 현지 해외기업에 지원하는 경우: 북미 기준

a) 유선전화(일반전화):

→ 지역번호(area code)[5] – 전화번호(phone #)

(Ex) 캐나다 밴쿠버에 거주하는 지원자가 토론토 소재 회사에 지원하는 경우:

604 – * * * – * * * *

→ 지원자와 다른 지역에 있는 회사에 지원할 때 당연히 자신의 거주지역인 밴쿠버 지역번호(604)를 기재한다.

(Ex) 캐나다 밴쿠버에 거주하는 지원자가 밴쿠버 소재 회사에 지원하는 경우:

604 – * * * – * * * *

→ 지원자와 같은 지역에 있는 회사에 지원할 때에도 자신의 거주지역인 밴쿠버 지역번호(604)를 기재한다.

b) 무선전화(휴대전화):

→ 지역번호 – 휴대폰번호

(Ex) 캐나다 밴쿠버에 거주하는 지원자가 **현지 휴대폰**으로 밴쿠버 및 토론토 소재 회사에 지원하는 경우:

604 – * * * – * * * *

(Ex) 캐나다 밴쿠버에 거주하는 지원자가 **현지 휴대폰**으로 미국[6] 소재 회사에 지원하는 경우:

1 – 604 – * * * – * * * *

(Ex) 캐나다 밴쿠버에 거주하는 지원자가 **한국 휴대폰**으로 캐나다 소재 회사에 지원하는 경우:

+ 한국국가번호(82) - 휴대폰번호

+ 82 - 10 – * * ** – * * * *

→ 여기서도 휴대폰 번호를 적을 때 앞자리 숫자 <0>을 제외하고 기재해야 한다.
(단 한국통신사에 로밍 서비스를 신청해 놓은 조건이어야 한다)

---

5) 북미 지역번호는 세자리(200~900) 번호이다.

6) 미국에서는 전 지역에서, 다시 말해 다른 지역에서 뿐만 아니라 동일한 지역 내에서도 1번을 눌러야 하는 통화시스템을 갖는다.

II. Receiver's information: 수신자 이름과 주소 – Optional

→ <Header> 밑으로 한 줄 아래에 기재[7)]

지원하는 회사와의 확인과정을 거쳐 (철자가 틀리지 않도록) 수신자의 정확한 이름과 주소를 적는다. 수신자의 직함(title)을 아는 경우에는 수신자 이름 뒤에 쉼표(,)를 찍고 직함을 쓰거나 공간의 여유가 있을 때에는 수신자 이름 바로 아랫줄에 직함을 적는다.

Robert Roy, Head of Human Resources

Robert Roy
Head of Human Resources

첫째 줄에 수신자의 이름(+직함)을 적고, 줄을 바꿔서 주소를 쓰는데 국제우편으로 보낼 때 국가명은 마지막 행에 독립해서 쓴다.

Gordon Soo, Hiring Manager
1234 Highway Road[8)]
Vancouver BC, V1V 1V1
Canada

또한 첫째 줄에 수신자의 이름을 쓰고 그 밑에 회사명을 쓰고 줄을 바꾸어 주소를 쓰기도 하는데 국내우편인 경우 국가명은 생략한다.

Mr. Edward A. Martins
New York Trading Co., LTD
250 Fifth Avenue
New York NY, V1V 1V1

---

7) head 작성 후 아래로 <몇 줄을 띄우는가?>에 대한 정해진 규칙은 없다. 일반적으로 쓰고자 하는 전체 내용의 분량을 고려해서 정하는 것이 좋다.

8) **도로주소(street address)**는 "highway", "way", "road", "street", "avenue", "place", "drive" 등과 같이 다양하게 표기된다.
Examples of local roads: Lougheed Highway, Cape Horn Ave, Cape Horn Place, Woodland Drive, Kingsway, Highway 1, No 1 Road, 5th Street, 108 Avenue.

III. Date: 발신 날짜

→ 수신자의 주소 밑으로 한 줄 아래에 기재

<월 일, 년도>의 형태로 쓴다.

(Ex) July 26, 2022

이때 Aug, Sept, Oct와 같이 약어로 표시한다든지 혹은 숫자만으로 날짜를 기재하는 것, 예를 들어 5/2/01 과 같은 표기는 피해야 한다.

IV. Salutation: 인사말

→ 날짜 밑으로 한 줄 아래에 기재

받는 사람 이름을 기재할 때 보편적으로 이름 앞에 Dear를 쓰고, 이름 뒤에 콜론(:)을 붙이거나 콤마(,)를 붙인다. 콜론은 매우 격식 있는 표현으로서 상대방이 높은 직위에 있거나 중요한 이메일을 처음 보낼 때 사용한다.

① 수신자(인사담당자)의 성별과 이름을 아는 경우, Dear 다음에 경칭(Mr. Mrs. Miss. Ms,)을 쓰고 이름을 기재한다. 이때 가급적 fall name(전체 이름)을 기재하는 것이 좋다.

Dear Mr.[9] Gordon Soo: (O)

Dear Mr. Soo: (△)

② 수신자(인사담당자)의 성별과 결혼유무[10]에 대해 모르는 경우, Dear 다음에 상대방의 전체 이름을 기재한다.

Dear Alex Park:

③ 수신자(인사담당자)의 이름을 모르는 경우, Dear 다음에 직함 예를 들어 "Dear Hiring Manager:" 혹은 "Dear Hiring Team:"이라고 적는다. 또한 Dear 다음에 "Sir/Madam:"을 쓰기도 하고, "To Whom It May Concern:"이라고 기재할 수도 있다[11].

9) 영국에서는 Mr/Ms 뒤에 마침표를 찍지 않는다.

10) 상대방이 여성인 경우 'Miss' 나 'Mrs' 보다 'Ms'라는 경칭을 사용할 것을 추천한다.

11) 근래에는 <Dear Sir>, <Dear Madam>, <To Whom It May Concern>과 같은 표현들은 예전에 비해 덜 활용된다.

Dear Hiring Manager:

Dear Hiring Team:

Dear Sir:

Dear Madam:[12)]

To Whom It May Concern:

V. Introduction paragraph: 서론

→ 인사말 밑으로 한 줄 아래에 기재

본인에 대한 소개, 지원목적, 희망직종 및 지원경로 등을 언급하면서 자신을 부각시킬 수 있는 중요한 단락이다. 공손하면서도 간결하게 작성할 것을 권한다.

Here you would introduce yourself, or the reason for your letter. **The first paragraph is the most important.** You will be competing against many other candidates and job-seekers, and you will want to have your letter stand out among the others. In this paragraph, you will introduce yourself, and explain the purpose of why you are writing, and your career goals. You will want to be polite but concise.

VI. Body (2 or 3 paragraphs): 본론

→ 서론 밑으로 한 줄 아래에 기재

학력과 경력, 업무관련 역량 강조: 지원자의 과거 업무성과와 경력 및 관련업무 능력을 설득력 있게 부각시킨다. 업무와의 연관성이 가장 높은 문단으로서 이력서에 기재된 내용을 반복하기 보다는 자신이 다양한 경력과 능력을 갖춘, 해당업무에 적합한 인재라는 점을 밝히는 것이 좋다.

Describe your skills and qualifications. This includes any relevant education, volunteer or work experiences. In order to make you a good candidate for the job, highlight the positive aspects of yourself. Be careful not to simply repeat what is on your resume. Instead, share informa-

12) "Dear Madam:"의 경우 북미에서 사용되지 않는다.

tion that cannot be easily written into your resume, such as the time you showed leadership or initiative by doing something unique in a project, or a time that you faced a challenge that energized you.

VII. Concluding paragraph: 결론

→ 본론 밑으로 한 줄 아래에 기재

자신의 편지를 읽어준 상대방에게 정중하게 감사함을 표하면서 채용에 대한 자신의 관심과 열정 나아가 면접 기회를 요청하는 것으로 마무리한다.

In your concluding paragraph, thank the reader (hiring manager) for taking time to read your letter. Show your enthusiasm and confidence by inviting the reader of your letter to contact you. Remind the reader of your excitement or enthusiasm for applying for the job.

VIII. Closing: 끝인사

→ 결론 밑으로 한 줄 아래에 기재

본문 내용을 작성한 후에 인사처럼 쓰는 말이다. 특별한 뜻은 없고 '감사합니다' 정도로 이해하면 된다.

Sincerely, Sincerely yours, Yours sincerely,	일반적인 비즈니스 서신의 경우
Truly yours, Yours truly,	격식을 차려야 하는 비즈니스 서신의 경우
Respectfully, Respectfully yours, Yours respectfully,	정부관료나 대학교수에게 보내는 비즈니스 서신의 경우
Best regards, Regards, Best wishes,	친분이 있는 직장 동료나 부하직원에게 보내는 비즈니스 서신의 경우

또한 끝인사 아래에는 이메일이 아닌 경우, 자필서명(signature)을 할 수 있는 공간을 남겨야 한다.

IX. Signature and Sender's Name: 자필서명과 지원자 이름

→ 끝인사 밑으로 한 줄을 띄우기도 하고 경우에 따라 두 줄을 띄우기도 한다.

끝인사 밑에 자필서명을 하는 경우 그것을 위한 충분한 공간을 남긴다.

(Ex) Yours truly,

Winnie Mah (signature)
Winnie Mah (sender's name)

X. Enclosure: 동봉물

→ 지원자 이름 다음에 4줄 띄고 기재

우편으로 자기소개서를 보낼 때 이력서를 동봉하는 경우에는 <Enclosure>라고 적은 후, Enclosure 다음에 colon(:)을 붙이고 동봉하는 문서제목을 쓴다.

(Ex) Enclosure: resume

또 다른 방식으로는, 동봉하는 문서가 1개인 경우에는 그 문서가 어떤 종류이든 상관없이 <Enclosure> 혹은 <Enclosure: 1> 이라고 쓰면 된다.

(Ex) Enclosure
(Ex) Enclosure: 1

동봉하는 문서가 2개 이상인 경우에는 <Enclosures:>라고 적은 후 동봉한 모든 문서들의 제목들을 적는다.

(Ex) Enclosures:
Resume
Application Form

(Ex) Enclosures: Resume, Application Form

또한 <Enclosures:>라고 적은 후 동봉문서의 개수만 적어도 가능하다.

(Ex) Enclosures: 2

Part 5 영작연습

다음 문장을 영작하시오.

1. 제 주소는 서울시 용산구 남영동 90-2번지입니다.

→ ______________________________

2. 저는 2000년 3월 15일에 태어났습니다.

→ ______________________________

2-① 저는 2000년 3월에 태어났습니다.

→ ______________________________

2-② 저는 2000년 3월 15일 월요일에 태어났습니다.

→ ______________________________

3. 저는 2017년 3월 한성여자고등학교에 입학했습니다.

→ ______________________________

<enter>

4. 저는 2018년에 성신여자고등학교로 전학하여 2019년 2월에 졸업했습니다.

→ ______________________________

____

<transfer / graduate>

5. 저는 같은 해 3월 협성대학에 입학하였습니다.

→ ______________________________

6. 저는 대학교 2학년 때 1년 휴학했습니다.

→ ______________________________

<out of school>

7. 저는 대학교 2학년 때 결핵에 걸려서 1년 휴학했습니다.

→ ______________________________

<tuberculosis>

7-① 저는 대학교 3학년 때 집안형편이 어려워서 2년 휴학했습니다.

→ ______________________________

<financial difficulty>

8. 가족구성원은 저를 포함해서 4명입니다.

→ ______________________________

<there are / including>

9. 저는 외향적입니다.

→ ______________________________

<extroverted>

9-① 저는 내성적입니다.

→ ______________________________

<introverted>

10. 저는 2005년에 협성대학교 영어동아리 회장으로 일했습니다.

→ ______________________________

<President>

Part 6 정답과 해설

1. 제 주소는 서울시 용산구 남영동 90-2번지입니다.
→ My address is 90-2, Namyoung-dong, Youngsan-ku, Seoul.

2. 저는 2000년 3월 15일에 태어났습니다.
→ I was born **on** March 15**,** 2000.
= I was born **on** March 15**th,** 2000.
* 날짜 앞에 on을 붙이고, 날짜와 년도 사이에 쉼표를 붙인다.

2-① 저는 2000년 3월에 태어났습니다.
→ I was born **in** March 2000.
* 달 앞에 in을 붙이고, 달과 년도만 있는 경우 중간에 쉼표를 붙이지 않는다.

2-② 저는 2000년 3월 15일 월요일에 태어났습니다.
→ I was born **on** Monday**,** March 15**,** 2000.
* 요일 앞에 on을 붙이고, 요일과 날짜 그리고 날짜와 년도 중간에 쉼표를 붙인다.

3. 저는 2017년 3월 한성여자고등학교에 입학했습니다.
<enter>
→ I **entered** Hansung Girl's High School in March 2017.
= I **began** Hansung Girl's High School in March 2017.

4. 저는 2018년에 성신여자고등학교로 전학하여 2019년 2월에 졸업했습니다.
<transfer / graduate>
→ **In 2018**, I transferred to Sungshin Girl's High School, and graduated in February 2019.
= I transferred to Sungshin Girl's High School **in 2018**, and graduated in February 2019.
* 수식어구(in 2018)는 고정된 자리가 없기 때문에 문장의 앞이나 뒤 혹은 중간에 모두 위치할 수 있다.

5. 저는 같은 해 3월 협성대학에 입학하였습니다.
→ **That same March**, I entered (began) Hyupsung University.
= **In March of that year**, I entered (began) Hyupsung University.

6. 저는 대학교 2학년 때 1년 휴학했습니다.
<out of school>

<미국식 표현>

= I was out of school for one year **when I was a sophomore in university.**

<캐나다식 표현>

I was out of school for one year **when I was in my second year of university.**
= I was out of school for one year **when I was in the second year at university.**
= I was out of school for one year **when I was a second-year student at university.**

** **참고**: 위 문맥에서 다음과 같이 휴학사유를 함께 적는 것이 좋다.

Examples:

- I was out of school for one year **due to an illness.**
- I was out of school for one year **due to an injury from a baseball.**
- I was out of school for one year **when I was given the opportunity to live abroad for one year.**

7. 저는 대학교 2학년 때 결핵에 걸려서 1년 휴학했습니다.

<tuberculosis>

→ I was **out of school** for one year **when I was a sophomore in university** because I got tuberculosis. - 미국식 표현
→ I was out of school for one year **when I was in my second year of university** because I got tuberculosis. - 캐나다식 표현
= I was out of school for one year **when I was in the second year at university** because I got tuberculosis.
= I was out of school for one year **when I was a second-year student at university** because I got tuberculosis.

** **대체 가능한 표현**

① I was out of school for one year when I was in the second year at university **because I was recovering from tuberculosis.**

② I was out of school for one year when I was in the second year **because I was recovering from an illness.** *(if you do not want to say what illness).*

7-① 저는 대학교 3학년 때 집안 형편이 어려워서 2년 휴학했습니다.

<financial difficulty>

→ I was **out of school** for two years **when I was a junior in university,** because my family had a financial difficulty. (△O))
= I was **out of school** for two years **when I was in my third year of university,** because my family had a financial difficulty. (△O)

**** 보충설명**: '경제적 어려움'을 의미하는 다음과 같은 표현들은 올바른 문장이다:

→ I was out of school for two years when I was a junior in university due to (=because of) **a financial difficulty**. (O)

= I was out of school for two years when I was a junior in university due to **a financial hardship.** (O)

* <financial> 앞에 <a>를 생략해도 가능하다.

= I was out of school for two years when I was a junior in university due to **financial constraints.** (O)

****보충설명**: <휴학하다>를 의미하는 다양한 표현들:

<out of school> **<do (does) not attend>** **<take a break from>** **<My attendance ... be interrupted>**

Examples:

I was **out of school** for two years when I was a junior in university due to financial difficulty.
= I **did not attend** university for two years when I was a junior due to (a) financial difficulty.
= **My attendance** in university **was interrupted** when I was a junior due to financial difficulty.
= I **took a break from** university in my third year, to work full-time, before returning to school.[13)]
- *(This is implied that there was some financial difficulty, or a need to work)*

8. 가족구성원은 저를 포함해서 4명입니다.

<there are / including>

→ There are four members in my family, including myself.
= My family has four members, including **myself.**
= My family has four members, including **me.**
≠ My family members are four of us including me. (X)

9. 저는 외향적입니다.

<extroverted>

→ I am **extroverted.**
= I am **an extrovert.**

---

13) Another Example: <고등학교(대학교) 때 1년 휴학했습니다.>

→ I was **out of school** for one year during high school(university) because ...
= I **did not attend** high school for one year because ...
= **My attendance** in high school **was interrupted** for one year because ...
= I **took a break from** high school for one year because ...

→ I am outgoing. (△) (비격식체 표현)

9-① 저는 내성적입니다.

<introverted>

→ I am **introverted.**

= I am **an introvert.**

→ I am reserved. (△) (비격식체 표현)

10. 저는 2005년에 협성대학교 영어동아리 회장으로 일했습니다.

<President>

→ I worked as President of the English Club at Hyupsung University in 2005.

* **참고:** 'President'가 title(직함)이기 때문에 대문자(P)로 시작해야 하고, 'President' 앞에 관사를 생략한다.

Fundamental Exercises

1. 영문 비즈니스 문서의 기본 양식 중에서 업무용으로 사용되는 대표서식을 고르시오.

① Semi-Block Form
② Indented Form
③ Block Form
④ Simplified Form

2. 다음 중 커버레터의 내용으로 적합하지 않은 것을 선택하시오.

① skills
② sexual orientation
③ work experiences
④ qualifications

3. 다음 문장을 읽고 밑줄친 부분에 해당하는 구문을 영어로 적으시오.

I was ________________ for two years when I was a junior in university due to a financial difficulty. (저는 대학교 3학년 때 경제적인 어려움 때문에 2년 휴학했습니다.)

→ ________________________________

4. 공식문서에 적합하지 않은 끝인사는 무엇인가?

① Sincerely yours,
② Yours truly,
③ Respectfully,
④ Best regards,

5. 국내 거주자가 해외기업에 지원할 때 커버레터 작성과정에서 필요한 지원자의 핸드폰 번호(010 – 1234 – 5678)를 알맞게 표기하시오.

→ ________________________________

Part 7 Example of a Properly Formatted Cover Letter

Header (발신자 정보)

수신자 정보

발신 날짜

인사말

저는 매사추세츠 대학교 경영대학에서 마케팅을 전공하고 커뮤니케이션을 부전공하는 4학년 학부생입니다. Amy Wright에 의해 소개된 것처럼, MC Agency의 광고 및 홍보에 대한 접근 방식에 깊은 감명을 받았습니다. 고객이 가질 수 있는 모든 문제들을 해결하기 위해 다양한 전략을 만들어 내는 MC Agency의 능력은 인상적입니다. 특히 온라인 미디어와 관련해서, 저는 혁신적인 마케팅 전략과 전통적인 방법을 결합하는 것에 믿음이 있습니다. 저의 마케팅 접근 방식은 항상 고객 중심적이며 성과에 기반을 둘 것입니다. 이러한 점을 염두에 두고, 저는 MC Agency의 마케팅 보조 직무 채용면접에 불러주실 것을 부탁드리고자 글을 적습니다.

지난 2년간, 저는 소도시의 야생동물을 구조하고 재활치료하는 비영리 기업, Urban Animal Rescue에서 자원봉사자로 일했습니다. 그들의 마케팅 컨설턴트로서, 저는 구조의 임무에 대해 대중을 교육하기 위한 마케팅 전략을 평가하고 이행하는 것을 도왔습니다. 틱톡, 인스타그램, 유튜브를 통해 마케팅 팀은 구조교육 캠페인을 더 젊은 청중들에게 소개할 수 있었습니다. 저는 소셜 미디어 게시물, 블로그와 뉴스레터의 참여를 향상시키기 위해 콘텐츠 팀과 함께 일하는 데 많은 시간을 보냈습니다.

커뮤니케이션 부전공은 마케팅 분야에서 제 업무와 교육의 자산이 되었습니다. 그것은 저로 하여금 대중의 심리에 미치는 뉴미디어의 영향을 받아들이고 인식하게 해 주었습니다. 모든 플랫폼은 그 기반 청중이 있기에, 미디어 그 자체뿐만 아니라 청중을 이해함으로써 제가 광고에 대한 접근을 더 잘하고 더 효과적으로 할 수 있게 되었습니다. 더불어, 마케팅에 대한 지식과 열정을 가지고, 저는 분석과 창의적인 문제해결을 통해 예상치 못한 방법으로 성과를 도출했습니다.

MC Agency와 함께 일할 수 있는 기회를 가지게 되어 매우 기쁘며, 제가 회사에 기여할 수 있는 방법들에 대해 선생님과 이야기를 나눌 기회를 가지고 싶습니다. 감사드리며 연락을 기다리겠습니다.

끝인사,

자필서명과 발신자 이름

이력서 동봉

<English Words and Idioms>

area code　지역번호
recruiter　채용 담당자

senior　4학년 (freshman : 1학년, sophomore : 2학년, junior : 3학년)
College of Business (Administration)　경영대학
major in　~을 전공하다
minor　부전공
be impressed with　~에 감명 받다
result　성과
approach (to)　(~에 대한) 접근방식
advertising and promotion　광고와 홍보
present　제시(소개)하다
diverse　다양한
strategy　전략
form　만들어내다
tackle the problem　문제를 해결하다
impressive　인상적인
when it comes to　~과 관련해서, ~에 대해서
blend A with B　A와 B를 결합하다.
innovative　혁신적인
method　방법
client-focused　고객중심의
result-based　성과에 기반하는
with 목적어 in mind　~을 염두에 두고
request　부탁하다
Marketing Assistant position　마케팅 보조 직무

non-profit　비영리적인
rescue　구조하다 / 구조
rehabilitate　재활치료하다
small urban　소도시의
wildlife　야생동물
evaluate　평가하다
implement　이행하다
strategy　전략
public　대중, 일반 사람들
mission　임무
be able to　~ 할 수 있다.
rescue's educational campaign　구조 교육 캠페인

audience 청중
spend time ~ing ~하는 데 시간을 보내다
improve 향상시키다.
engagement 참여
social media posts 소셜 미디어 게시물

asset (to) ~의 자산, 재산
work 업무
allow A to A가 ~하도록 허락하다
embrace 받아들이다, 수용하다
appreciate 인식하다, 알아보다
impact (on) ~ 에 미치는 영향
psyche 심리, 마음
base audience 기반 청중 (고정적인 청중)
not only A, but (also) B A뿐만 아니라 B도
effective 효과적인
together 더불어
passion 열정
yield 도출하다, 산출하다
unexpected 예상치 못한
analysis 분석
problem-solving 문제해결

be pleased with ~에 기뻐하다
the ways in which - how
contribute (to) : ~에 기여하다
look forward to ~ing : ~하기를 고대하다
→ look forward to hearing from you soon (곧 소식이 있기를 고대합니다 = 연락을 기다리겠습니다)
enclosure 동봉된 것
résumé 이력서

Part 8 영작연습

다음 문장을 영작하시오.

자기소개서

→ ______________________________

발신자(지원자) 이름 및 주소

(예: 박 제임스

02609 대한민국 서울시 동대문구 답십리로 210)

→ ______________________________

____

연락처

(예: redhouse@hanmail.net

010 – 5678 – 1234)

→ ______________________________

____

발신 날짜

(예: 2022년 10월 13일)

→ ______________________________

담당자 귀하

→ ______________________________

1. The First Paragraph

저는 매사추세츠 대학교 경영대학에서 마케팅을 전공하고 커뮤니케이션을 부전공하는 4학년 학부생입니다.

→ ____

____

<senior / College of Business / majoring in / with / minor>

Amy Wright에 의해 소개된 것처럼, 저는 MC Agency의 광고 및 홍보에 대한 접근 방식에 깊은 감명을 받았습니다.

→ ____

____

<be impressed with / approach to / advertising and promotion / as presented by>

고객이 가질 수 있는 모든 문제들을 해결하기 위해 다양한 전략을 만들어 내는 MC Agency의 능력은 인상적입니다.

→ ____

____

<to form / diverse / tackle all the problem / may / impressive>

특히 온라인 미디어와 관련해서, 저는 혁신적인 마케팅 전략과 전통적인 방법을 결합하는 것에 믿음이 있습니다.

→ ____

____

<when it comes to / believe in / blend A with B / innovative / methods>

저의 마케팅 접근 방식은 항상 고객 중심적이며 성과에 기반을 둘 것입니다.

→ ____

<approach to / client-focused / result-based>

이러한 점을 염두에 두고, 저는 MC Agency의 마케팅 보조 직무 (채용)면접에 불러주실 것을 부탁드리고자 글을 적습니다.

→ ____

____

<with 목적어 in mind / request an invitation to interview / Marketing Assistant position>

2. The Second Paragraph

지난 2년간, 저는 소도시의 야생동물을 구조하고 재활 치료하는 비영리 기업, Urban Animal Rescue에서 자원봉사자로 일했습니다.

→ ____

____

<non-profit / that / rehabilitate / small urban wildlife>

그들의 마케팅 컨설턴트로서, 저는 구조의 임무에 대해 대중을 교육하기 위한 마케팅 전략을 평가하고 이행하는 것을 도왔습니다.

→ ____

____

<implement / strategies / the public / mission>

틱톡, 인스타그램, 유튜브를 통해 마케팅 팀은 구조교육 캠페인을 더 젊은 청중들에게 소개할 수 있었습니다.

→ ____

____

<through / be able to / rescue's educational campaign / audience>

저는 소셜 미디어 게시물, 블로그와 뉴스레터의 참여를 향상시키기 위해 콘텐츠 팀과 함께 일하는 데 많은 시간을 보냈습니다.

→ ____

____

<spend time ~ing / engagement from / social media posts>

3. The Third Paragraph

커뮤니케이션 부전공은 마케팅(분야)에서 제 업무와 교육의 자산이 되었습니다.

→ ____

<my communications / asset to / work>

그것은 저로 하여금 대중의 심리에 미치는 뉴미디어의 영향을 받아들이고 인식하게 해 주었습니다.

→ ____

____

<allow A to ~ / embrace / impact (on) / public psyche>

모든 플랫폼은 그 기반 청중이 있기에, 미디어 그 자체뿐만 아니라 청중을 이해함으로써, 제가 광고에 대한 접근을 더 잘하고 더 효과적으로 할 수 있게 되었습니다.

→ ____

____

<base audience / and / by / not only A , but (also) B / be able to / better and more effective with / approach to>

더불어, 마케팅에 대한 지식과 열정을 가지고, 저는 분석과 창의적인 문제해결을 통해 예상치 못한 방법으로 성과를 도출했습니다.

→ ____

____

<together / with / passion in / yield / results / unexpected / through / problem-solving>

4. The Fourth Paragraph

MC Agency와 함께 일할 수 있는 기회를 가지게 되어 매우 기쁘며, 제가 회사에 기여할 수 있는 방법들에 대해 선생님과 이야기를 나눌 기회를 가지고 싶습니다.

→ ____

____

<be pleased with / welcome the opportunity / speak with / the ways in which= how / contribute to>

감사드리며 연락을 기다리겠습니다.

→ ____________________

<look forward to ~ing>

끝인사,

→ __________

발신자 이름

→ __________

이력서 동봉

→ __________

자기소개서
→ Cover Letter

지원자 이름 및 주소
(예: 박 제임스
02609 대한민국 서울시 동대문구 답십리로 210)
→ James Park
210, Dapsimni-ro, Dongdaemun-gu
Seoul, 02609
Korea

연락처
(예: redhouse@hanmail.net
010 – 5678 - 1234)
→ redhouse@hanmail.net
+82-10-5678-1234

발신 날짜
(예: 2022년 10월 13일)
→ October 13, 2022

담당자 귀하
→ To Whom It May Concern:

1. The First Paragraph

저는 매사추세츠 대학교 경영대학에서 마케팅을 전공하고 커뮤니케이션을 부전공하는 4학년 학부생입니다.

<senior / College of Business / majoring in / with / minor>

→ I am a senior at the College of Business in the University of Massachusetts majoring in marketing with a communications minor.

Amy Wright에 의해 소개된 것처럼, 저는 MC Agency의 광고 및 홍보에 대한 접근 방식에 깊은 감명을 받았습니다.

<be impressed with / approach to / advertising and promotion / as presented by>

→ I was very impressed with MC Agency's approach to advertising and promotion **as presented by Amy Wright.**

= **As (it was) presented by Amy Wright**, I was very impressed with MC Agency's approach to advertising and promotion.

고객이 가질 수 있는 모든 문제들을 해결하기 위해 다양한 전략을 만들어 내는 MC Agency의 능력은 인상적입니다.

<to form / diverse / tackle all the problem / may / impressive>

→ MC Agency's ability to form diverse strategies to tackle all the problems a client(customer) **may** have is impressive.

* 위 문맥에서 <may> 대신에 <can>을 써도 가능하지만 원어민의 시각으로는 <may>를 쓰는 것이 더 적합한 표현이라고 한다.

= MC Agency's ability to form diverse strategies to tackle all the problems a client may have is **intriguing.**

특히 온라인 미디어와 관련해서, 저는 혁신적인 마케팅 전략과 전통적인 방법을 결합하는 것에 믿음이 있습니다.

<when it comes to / believe in / blend A with B / innovative / methods>

→ **Especially when it comes to onlinie media,** I believe in blending innovative marketing strategies with traditional methods.

= I believe in blending innovative marketing strategies with traditional methods, **especially when it comes to online media.**

저의 마케팅 접근 방식은 항상 고객 중심적이며 성과에 기반을 둘 것입니다.

<approach to / client-focused / result-based>

→ My approach to marketing will always be client-focused, and results-based.

이러한 점을 염두에 두고, 저는 MC Agency의 마케팅 보조 직무 (채용)면접에 불러주실 것을 부탁드리고자 글을 적습니다.

<with 목적어 in mind / request an invitation to interview / Marketing Assistant position>

→ With this in mind, I am writing to request an **invitation to interview for** a Marketing Assistant position at(with) MC Agency.

= With this in mind, I am writing to request an **interview for the position of** Marketing Assistant at(with) MC Agency.

= With this in mind, I am writing to request **for** an **interview for** a Marketing Assistant position at(with) MC Agency.

* 지원자가 원하는 특정 직책이 'Marketing Assistant'이기 때문에 단어의 첫 레터를 대문자로 표기한다

= With this in mind, I am writing **to ask for** an **invitation to interview for** a Marketing Assistant position at(with) MC Agency.

≠ With this in mind, I am writing to request an interview invitation for a Marketing Assistant position at(with) MC Agency. (X)

2. The Second Paragraph

지난 2년간, 저는 소도시의 야생동물을 구조하고 재활치료하는 비영리 기업, Urban Animal Rescue에서 자원봉사자로 일했습니다.

<non-profit / that / rehabilitate / small urban wildlife>

→ **For the past two years**, I worked as a volunteer at(for) Urban Animal Rescue, a non-profit company **that** rescues and rehabilitates small urban wildlife.

* 수식어구 (for the past two years)는 고정된 자리가 없기 때문에 문미에 와도 가능하다:

= I worked as a volunteer at(for) Urban Animal Rescue, a non-profit company **that** rescues and rehabilitates small urban wildlife **for the past two years**.

**** 원어민 설명:**

문법적으로 보았을 때 위 문장에서 우리가 사용할 수 있는 관계대명사로는 <that>과 <which> 둘 다 가능하지만, 이와 달리 원어민의 시각으로는 <which>가 아니라 <that>만 사용할 수 있다고 한다.

그들의 마케팅 컨설턴트로서, 저는 구조의 임무에 대해 대중을 교육하기 위한 마케팅 전략을 평가하고 이행하는 것을 도왔습니다.

<implement / strategies / the public / mission>

→ As their marketing consultant, I helped to evaluate and implement marketing strategies to educate the public about the rescue's mission.

틱톡, 인스타그램, 유튜브를 통해, 마케팅 팀은 구조교육 캠페인을 더 젊은 청중들에게 소개할 수 있었습니다.

<through / be able to / rescue's educational campaign / audience>

→ Through TikTok, Instagram, and Youtube, the marketing team was able to introduce the rescue's educational campaign to a younger audience.

저는 소셜 미디어 게시물, 블로그와 뉴스레터의 참여를 향상시키기 위해 콘텐츠 팀과 함께 일하는 데 많은 시간을 보냈습니다.

<spend time ~ing / engagement from / social media posts>

→ I spent a lot of time working with the content team to improve **engagement from** social media posts, blogs, and newsletters.

** **참고**: 'engagement' 뒤에 'about'이나 'of'를 쓰면 틀린 문장이 된다.

3. The Third Paragraph

커뮤니케이션 부전공은 마케팅(분야)에서 제 업무와 교육의 자산이 되었습니다.

<my communications / asset to / work>

→ My communications minor became an asset to my work and education in marketing.

= **My communication** minor became an asset to my work and education in marketing.

* 이 문장에서 marketing 앞에 전치사 at를 쓰면 틀린 문장이 된다.

≠ My communication minor became an asset to my work and education **at** marketing. (X)

그것은 저로 하여금 대중의 심리에 미치는 뉴미디어의 영향을 받아들이고 인식하게 해 주었습니다.

<allow A to ~ / embrace / impact on / public psyche>

→ It has allowed me to embrace and appreciate new media's impact on the public psyche.

모든 플랫폼은 그 기반 청중이 있기에, 미디어 그 자체뿐만 아니라 청중을 이해함으로써, 제가 광고에 대한 접근을 더 잘하고 더 효과적으로 할 수 있게 되었습니다.

<base audience / and / by / not only A , but (also) B / be able to / better and more effective with / approach to>

→ Every platform has its base audience, and by understanding not only the media itself, but its audience, I was able to become better and more effective **with** my approach to advertising.

* 위 문장에서 전치사 <with>를 <in>이나 <in regards to>로 바꾸어 써도 가능하다.

→ Every platform has its base audience, and by understanding not only the media itself, but its audience, I was able to become better and more effective **in** my approach to advertising.

= Every platform has its base audience, and by understanding not only the media itself, but its audience, I was able to become better and more effective **in regards to** my approach to advertising.

더불어, 마케팅에 대한 지식과 열정을 가지고, 저는 분석과 창의적인 문제해결을 통해 예상치 못한 방법으로 성과를 도출했습니다.

<together / with / passion in / yield / results / unexpected / through / problem-solving>

→ Together, with my knowledge and passion **in** marketing, I have yielded results in unexpected ways through analysis and creative problem-solving.

= Together, with my knowledge and passion **for** marketing, I have yielded results in unexpected ways through analysis and creative problem-solving.

* 이 문맥에서 passion 다음에 전치사 of를 쓰면 틀린 문장이 된다.

4. The Fourth Paragraph

MC Agency와 함께 일할 수 있는 기회를 가지게 되어 매우 기쁘며, 제가 회사에 기여할 수 있는 방법들에 대해 선생님과 이야기를 나눌 기회를 가지고 싶습니다.

<be pleased with / welcome the opportunity / speak with / the ways in which = how / contribute to>

→ I am very pleased with **having** the opportunity to work with MC Agency, and I **welcome** the opportunity to speak with you about the ways in which I can contribute to the company.

= I am very pleased with **having** the opportunity to work with MC Agency, and I **would like to have** the opportunity to speak with you about how I can contribute to the company.

* 위 문장에서 **<with>**와 **<the>** 사이에 **<having>**를 생략하는 것도 가능하다:

= I am very pleased with the opportunity to work with MC Agency, and I welcome the opportunity to speak with you about the ways in which I can contribute to the company.

* <I am very pleased with the opportunity to work with MC Agency, and I welcome the opportunity to speak with you about **the ways**. + I can contribute to the company **in the ways**.>

= I am very **excited to have** the opportunity **to** speak with you about the ways in which I **may be able to** contribute to your company.

감사드리며 연락을 기다리겠습니다.

<look forward to ~ing>

→ Thank you and I look forward to hearing from you soon.

= I am, therefore, looking forward to hearing from you soon.
Thank you.

끝인사,

→ Sincerely,

발신자 이름

→ *James Park*
James Park

이력서 동봉

→ Enclosure: resume

= Enclosure

= Enclosure: 1

Part 10 Final Draft

Cover Letter

James Park
210, Dapsimni-ro, Dongdaemun-gu
Seoul, 02609
Korea
redhouse@hanmail.net
+82-10-5678-1234

Recruiter's Name
Campus Recruiter
MC Agency
265 Park Street[14)]
Boston MA, 02116
USA

October 13, 2022

Dear Campus Recruiter:

I am a senior at the College of Business in the Univetsity of Massachusetts majoring in marketing with a communications minor. I was very impressed with MC Agency's approach to advertising and promotion as presented by Amy Wright. MC Agency's ability to form diverse strategies to tackle all the problems a client may have is impressive. I believe in blending innovative marketing strategies with traditional methods, especially when it comes to online media. My approach to marketing will always be client-focused, and results-based. With this in mind, I am writing to request an invitation to interview for a Marketing Assistant position at MC Agency.

14) street address (company address)

For the past two years, I worked as a volunteer at Urban Animal Rescue, a non-profit company that rescues and rehabilitates small urban wildlife. As their marketing consultant, I helped to evaluate and implement marketing strategies to educate the public about the rescue's mission. Through TikTok, Instagram, and Youtube, the marketing team was able to introduce the rescue's educational campaign to a younger audience. I spent a lot of time working with the content team to improve engagement from social media posts, blogs, and newsletters.

My communications minor is an asset to my work and education in marketing. It has allowed me to embrace and appreciate new media's impact on the public psyche. Every platform has its base audience, and by understanding not only the media itself, but its audience, I was able to become better and more effective with my approach to advertising. Together, with my knowledge and passion for marketing, I have yielded results in unexpected ways through analysis and creative problem-solving.

I am very pleased with having the opportunity to work with MC Agency, and I welcome the opportunity to speak with you about the ways in which I can contribute to the company. Thank you and I look forward to hearing from you soon.

Sincerely,

James Park

James Park

Enclosure: resume

Fundamental Exercises

1. 다음 밑줄 친 구문(phrase)의 뜻을 적으시오.

> Especially when it comes to onlinie media, I believe in blending innovative marketing strategies with traditional methods.

→ ____________________

2. 다음 문장을 읽고 밑줄 친 부분에 적합한 전치사를 적으시오.

> I was very impressed with MC Agency's approach ________ advertising and promotion as presented by Amy Wright.
> (Amy Wright에 의해 소개된 것처럼, 저는 MC Agency의 광고 및 홍보에 대한 접근 방식에 깊은 감명을 받았습니다.)

→ ____________________

3. 다음 문장을 읽고 밑줄 친 부분에 적합한 구문을 영어로 적으시오.

> I am a senior at the College of Business in the University of Massachusetts ________ ________ with a communications minor.
> (저는 매사추세츠 경영대학에서 마케팅을 전공하고 커뮤니케이션을 부전공하는 4학년 학부생입니다.)

→ ____________________

4. 다음 문장을 읽고 밑줄 친 부분에 들어갈 관계대명사를 고르시오.

> For the past two years, I worked as a volunteer at(for) Urban Animal Rescue, a non-profit company ________ rescues and rehabilitates small urban wildlife.

① which ② that ③ who ④ whom

5. 다음 문장을 읽고 밑줄 친 구문의 뜻을 선택하시오.

> MC Agency's ability to form diverse strategies to tackle all the problems a client may have is impressive.

① 모든 문제를 파악하다. ② 모든 문제를 수집하다.
③ 모든 문제를 찾아내다. ④ 모든 문제를 해결하다.

4장

국문 이력서

국문 이력서는 자기소개서와 더불어 채용과정에서 지원자가 준비해야 할 가장 중요한 서류이다. 예전에는 지원자가 자신이 원하는 회사에 이력서를 제출할 때, 일종의 표준화된 이력서 양식을 참고하여 작성하였다. 그러나 요즘에는 각 회사가 제공하고 있는 여러 형태의 다양한 온라인 이력서 양식이 있기 때문에 본인이 취업하고자 하는 특정 회사 양식에 맞추어 이력서를 작성해야 한다. 따라서 이력서 양식을 표준화하여 제시하기는 어렵지만, 구성이나 형식에 있어서의 차이만 있을 뿐 실질적으로 내용에 있어서 대동소이하다고 할 수 있다. 국문 이력서는 지원자의 학력이나 경력을 담당자에게 가장 객관적인 방식으로 보여주는 서류라고 할 수 있는데, 일반적으로 학력, 경력, 어학 및 자격사항 그리고 과외활동 등의 4가지로 이루어진다. 회사에 따라 추가되는 항목이 있을 수 있지만 위에서 언급한 4가지 항목이 주된 내용이라고 할 수 있다. 이력서를 작성하기 전, 지원자가 회사 홈페이지를 방문하여 채용과정에서 회사 측으로부터 특정한 요구사항이 있는지 혹은 작성법과 관련하여 특별한 지시가 있는지 확인해야 할 필요가 있다.

Part 1 국문 이력서 양식

<이력서>

사 진	성 명	
	생년월일	
	전화번호	
	이 메 일	
	주 소	

■ 학력사항

학 교 명	학업기간	전 공 명	비 고
	20 년 월 ~ 20 년 월		
	20 년 월 ~ 20 년 월		
	20 년 월 ~ 20 년 월		

■ 주요 경력사항

업체(기관)명	근무기간	직 위	담당업무
	20 년 월 ~ 20 년 월		
	20 년 월 ~ 20 년 월		

■ 어학 및 자격사항

자격명	취득일자	등급 및 점수	발급기관

■ 과외활동

활동기관	활동기간	역할	성과
	20 년 월 ~ 20 년 월		
	20 년 월 ~ 20 년 월		

위에 기재한 사항은 사실과 틀림이 없습니다.

20 년 월 일

지원자 : ________(인)

Part 2 국문 이력서 항목

지원자의 경력을 채용담당자에게 가장 객관적인 방법으로 보여주는 서류로서 앞에서 언급한 인적사항, 학력, 경력, 어학 및 자격사항, 과외활동으로 구성되어 있다. 지원자는 회사의 특정 양식에 따라 순서대로 기재하면 된다.

1. 인적사항

지원자의 이름과 주소, 주민등록번호 및 연락처 등에 대해 기재한다. 경우에 따라 희망취업조건 다시 말해 지원분야나 희망연봉에 대해 적는 항목이 제공되기도 한다.

2. 학력

인사담당자가 지원자의 이력서를 검토할 때 가장 주목하는 것은 학력과 경력이다. 처음 직장을 구하는 신입사원인 경우, 경력이 부족하기 때문에 강하게 어필할 수 있는 경험을 제시하지 않는 한 학력이 가장 중요한 항목으로 작용될 때가 많다. 이와 반대로 경력사원의 경우에는 업무와 직접적으로 연관된 최근의 경력이 학력보다 더 우선시되기 때문에 최근의 경력에 대해 구체적으로 기술하는 것이 좋다.

3. 경력

국문 이력서는 표 형태로 구성되기 때문에 실질적으로 지원자가 여유롭게 쓸 수 있는 공간이 부족하다. 이러한 이유에서, 지원자가 이전의 직장에서 어떤 일을 했는지에 대해 자세하게 기재하지 못하는 경우가 종종 있다. 그러나 기억해야 할 것은 회사의 입장에서 가장 궁금해 하는 것이 경력이라는 것이다. 신입사원인 경우에는 해당직무와 관련하여 예전에 했던 인턴이나 아르바이트 경험을 쓰면 되고, 경력사원인 경우에는 전 직장에서 담당했던 직무나 현장경험에 대해 기재하면 된다. 특히 경력직에 지원하는 지원자의 경우에는 인사담당자의 눈에 띌 수 있는 이력서를 작성하는 것이 중요한데, 예를 들면 자신의 스펙을 단순히 나열하는 것이 아니라 회사에서 필요로 하는 직무와 관련된 키워드 중심으로 해당 업무에서 어떤 성과를 얻었는지에 대해서 기재하는 것이 바람직하다.

4. 어학 및 자격사항

외국어나 컴퓨터 능력, 자격증, 상장 등 인사담당자의 관심을 끌만한 것들 중에서 해당 업무와 관련된 것을 중점적으로 기재한다. 외국어 능력과 관련하여, TOEIC, TOEIC Speaking, TEPS, OPIC 등 구체적인 공인 시험 점수를 적어야 하며 외국어 수준과 관련해서는, 상중하 대신에 '원어민 수준' 혹은 '일상회화 가능' 등 보다 상세하게 기재하는 것이 좋다. 컴퓨터 능력과 관련해서는, 회사에서 주로 사용하는 Microsoft Office (Excel, PowerPoint, Word) 능력이나 직무에서 필요로 하는 분석능력이나 프로그래밍 툴, 자료작성 능력 등에 대해 적는다. 또한 수상경력과 관련해서는, 포상의 구체적인 명칭뿐만 아니라 상을 수여한 기관까지 정확하게 기입하는 것이 내용의 신뢰성을 높일 수 있다.

5. 과외활동

예전에 언어 혹은 해당 업무와 연관된 연수 및 교육을 받았거나 봉사모임이나 동호회 등 특정단체에서 주도적인 역할을 한 경우 이에 대한 활동사항을 적는다.

5장

영문 이력서

영문 이력서는 영미권 기업에서 사용하는 입사서류 양식으로서 자기소개서와 더불어 채용 과정에서 지원자가 통과해야 할 가장 첫 단계라고 할 수 있는 서류이다. 커버레터가 희망직종이나 직위에 적합한 자신의 능력이나 자질에 대해 문장형식으로 작성하는 것이라면 이와 대조적으로 영문 이력서는 지원자의 학력과 경력 및 역량 등에 대해 간결하게 요점만 적는 것이라고 할 수 있다. 이때 알아두어야 할 것은, 대학을 갓 졸업한 지원자 다시 말해 경력이 없는 신입사원이 영어로 이력서를 작성하는 것을 <Personal History>라고 하고, 다양한 근무 경험이 있는 경력사원이 이력서를 작성하는 것을 <Resume>라고 칭한다는 점이다.

보편적으로 영문 이력서는 지원자 스스로 이력서의 순서나 양식을 정하여 작성하면 되는데 기업/회사에서 이력서 양식을 제공하는 경우에는 그 양식에 맞추어 이력서를 작성하면 된다. 영문 이력서는 보통 2장 이내로 작성하는 것을 권장하는데, 영문 이력서의 핵심이라 할 수 있는 최근 경력사항은 이력서 첫 페이지에 기재하고 나머지 항목들 예를 들어 학력, 특기 및 자격증, 과외활동 등은 그 다음 페이지에 기재하는 것이 바람직하다. 기재 순서와 관련하여 반드시 현재를 기준으로 과거로 거슬러 올라가면서 역순으로 명시해야 하며, 자신을 부각시킬 수 있는 수상경력이나 특이활동 등에 대해 언급할 때에는 간결하고 정제된 언어로 이를 보다 명확하게 작성함으로써 인사담당자로 하여금 읽어보기 쉽게 작성한다.

작성요령과 관련해서는, 일인칭 'I'는 가급적 사용하지 말고 동명사 대신 가능한 과거형 동사를 사용하고, 수동태 문장보다 능동태 문장을 활용할 것을 권장하며, 국문 이력서와 달리 자필서명은 따로 하지 않는다. 또한 글자크기는 최소 10pt가 넘도록 하여 가독성을 높이는 것이 좋고 일반적으로 서체는 Times New Roman을 사용하는 것이 바람직하다. 다음은 영문 이력서의 주요 구성요소들이다.

Part 1 General Outline of a Personal History (Resume)

1. **Header** 헤더 (발신자 정보- 이름, 주소, 전화번호 등)
2. **Career Objectives (Optional)** 희망 직종/ 지원 목표
3. **Education** 학력
4. **Work Experience** 경력
5. **Qualifications and Skills** 자격 및 특기사항
6. **License and Certificate** 면허 및 자격증
7. **Activities** 과외활동

* 참고 : Another Example of a different order:

1. Header: Sender's Information (Name, Address, Phone Number, etc)
2. Work Experience
3. Volunteer Experience
4. Special Skills (혹은 'Skills and Qualifications')
5. License and Certificate (Optional)
6. Education

⚑ 경우에 따라 <Intern Work>이라는 항목을 따로 추가할 수도 있다.

Part 2 How to Write a Personal History (Resume)

국문 이력서와 마찬가지로 영문 이력서의 경우에도 다양한 양식이 가능하지만 실제로는 지원하는 회사가 정해둔 양식에 따라 작성해야 하는 경우가 대부분이다. 따라서 이력서 양식을 표준화하여 제시하기는 어렵지만, 항목과 순서 혹은 형식에 있어서의 차이만 있을 뿐 실질적으로 내용에 있어서 대동소이하다고 할 수 있다. 일반적으로 영문 이력서에는 Header, 학력, 경력, 자격 및 특기사항, 면허 및 자격증 그리고 과외활동 등의 6가지로 이루어진다. 회사에 따라 추가되거나 누락되는 항목이 있을 수 있지만 위에서 언급한 6가지 항목이 주된 내용이라고 할 수 있다. 또한 커버레터와 마찬가지로 영문 이력서에서도 지원자의 개인 신상정보 예를 들어 나이나 성별, 결혼유무, 가족관계 등에 대해서는 기재할 필요가 없다.

1. **Header:** Sender's Information (헤더 – 발신자 정보)

지원자의 이름과 거주지 주소 및 연락처 등에 대해 명시한다. 이때 지원자 이름은 이력서의 제목과도 같은 역할을 하기 때문에 글자크기를 좀 더 크게 하거나 bold체로 강조함으로써 자신의 이름을 부각시킬 수 있다. 연락처 정보는 정해진 순서는 없지만 보편적으로 주소를 적고 난 후, 그 다음 줄에 이메일 주소 및 연락 가능한 전화번호(주로 휴대폰번호)를 기재한다.

Example:

Mary Grace Hwang
210, Dapsimni-ro, Dongdaemun-gu
Seoul, 02609
Korea
marygrace@hanmail.net
+82-10-8912-1234

2. Career Objectives (= Objectives) (희망직종 및 지원목표)

선택사항으로서 지원자가 원하는 희망직종(지원목표)이나 지원분야 나아가 입사 후 포부까지도 기재할 수 있다. 구인광고에 모집 분야가 명확하게 제시된 경우에는 희망직종을 그대로 명기하면 되지만 그렇지 않은 경우에는 이에 대한 자신의 의견을 두 줄 이내로 간단하게 작성하면 된다. 그 과정에서 유의해야 할 것은 지원자 자신이 요구하는 사항에 지나치게 초점을 맞추어 서술하다 보면 자칫 무례하게 보일 수 있기 때문에 자신의 요구사항보다는 자신의 강점과 지원목표 나아가 자신이 회사에 기여할 수 있는 내용을 중심으로 서술하는 것이 좋다.

Example:

I aim to obtain full-time employment in the field of Planning where I can progress with the department.
(저는 기획부서에서 정규직 일자리를 얻어서 그 부서와 함께 성장해 갈 수 있는 것을 목표로 하고 있습니다.)

* 지원자의 목표의식과 더불어 자신이 원하는 부서에서 그 조직과 함께 성장하고 싶다는 자신의 발전가능성과 포부를 드러내는 것이 좋다.

⬇

**** 기타 가능한 표현들:**

① I aim to find full-time employment in the Department of Planning, where I hope to apply my skills and knowledge, as well as grow within the department.

② I aim to find full-time employment in the Department of Planning, where I can use my skills and knowledge to it's full potential, and to progress with the department.

3. Education (학력)

구인회사로부터 특별한 요구사항이 없는 한 보통 최종 학력만을 기재한다. 기본적으로 대학교 이전의 학력은 작성할 필요가 없는데, 예를 들어 특수 목적고(외국어 고등학교/과학 고등학교)를 졸업했거나 고등학교 때 화려한 수상경력이 있는 경우에는 고등학교 학력을 기재하는 것이 도움이 되기도 한다. 최종학력을 적는 과정에서 학교명과 소재지 그리고 졸업년도(또는 재학년도)를 표기해야 하며 자신의 전공과 경우에 따라 부전공을 기재하기도 한다. 신입사원인 경우에는 경력이 빈약해 보일 수 있기 때문에 자신이 내세울만한 학점 및 장학금 수혜여부를 명시하는 것도 바람직하다.

① 졸업생인 경우

<사례 1 - more professional> :

Graduated from Simon Fraser University, Burnaby, 2016
B.B.A. in Business Administration,[15] minor in Architectural Engineering
With **a GPA of** 4.4/4.5
Awarded the Beedie School of Business Alumni Scholarship, March 2013

* 장학금을 받은 년도(2013)뿐만 아니라 달(March)까지 기재하는 것이 좋다.
* 장학금 수혜 여부와 관련하여, 일부교재에서는 이에 해당하는 동사로 <received>라고 표기하고 있으나, <awarded>가 이력서에 더 적합한 공식표현이다.

<사례1-① : less professional> :

Graduated from Simon Fraser University, Burnaby, 2016
Major: Business Administration
Minor: Architectural Engineering
With a GPA of 4.4/4.5
Awarded the Beedie School of Business Alumni Scholarship, March 2013

<사례 2 - more professional> :

Graduated from Hyupsung University, Hwaseong, February 2016
B.A. in English Language and Literature,[16] minor in Health Management

15) 경영학(경영학사)
대체 가능한 표현: Bisiness Administration in Bachelor of Business Administration

16) 영어영문학(문학사)

With **a GPA** of 4.3/4.5

Awarded a scholarship[17] March 2013

* 일반 장학금인 경우에는 scholarship 앞에 관사 a를 붙이고 특정 장학금인 경우에는 the를 붙인다[18]

<사례2-① : less professional> :

Graduated from Hyupsung University, Hwaseong, February 2016
Major: English Language and Literature
Minor: Health Management
With a GPA of 4.3/4.5
Awarded a scholarship March 2013

② 졸업예정자인 경우:

학위명을 표기한 후 <anticipated> 혹은 <degree to be awarded>를 기재하면 되는데 다음과 같은 두 가지 방식이 있다.

선택 1: 학위명 뒤에 **마침표를 찍고** 대문자 A로 시작하는 **Anticipated** 혹은 대문자 D로 시작하는 **Degree to be awarded**를 적는다.

<2022년 2월 협성대학 건축공학(공학사) 졸업예정>

Hyupsung University, Hwaseong, B.E. in Architectural Engineering**. Anticipated** February 2022

= Hyupsung University, Hwaseong, Architectural Engineering, Bachelor of Engineering**. Anticipated** February 2022

Hyupsung University, Hwaseong, B.E. in Architectural Engineering**. Degree to be awarded** February 2022

= Hyupsung University, Hwaseong, Architectural Engineering, Bachelor of Engineering**. Degree to be awarded** February 2022

대체 가능한 표현: English Language and Literature in Bachelor of Art

17) 대학 성적우수장학금을 영문으로 기재할 때 <university scholarship>, <merit scholarship>, <university scholarship for academic excellence>, <scholarship for academic excellence> 등과 같은 다양한 표현들이 있는데 이 중에서 가장 바람직한 표현은 <university scholarship>이다.

18) 예문: I was awarded **a** scholarship.
I was awarded **the** scholarship, Beedie School of Business Alumni Scholarship.
I was awarded **the** Beedie School of Business Alumni Scholarship.

🏴 **선택 2:** 학위명 뒤에 **쉼표를 찍고** 소문자 a로 시작하는 **anticipated** 혹은 소문자 d로 시작하는 **degree to be awarded** 를 적는다.

<2022년 2월 협성대학 국제통상학(경영학사) 졸업예정>

Hyupsung University, Hwaseong, B.B.A. in International Commerce**, anticipated** February 2022

= Hyupsung University, Hwaseong, International Commerce, Bachelor of Business Administration, **anticipated** February 2022

Hyupsung University, Hwaseong, B.B.A. in International Commerce**, degree to be awarded** February 2022

= Hyupsung University, Hwaseong, International Commerce, Bachelor of Business Administration, **degree to be awarded** February 2022

③ 재학생인 경우

소속학과 뒤에 **쉼표**를 적고 <**입학년도-present**> 라고 적는다. 또는 소속학과를 기재한 후 줄을 바꾸어 <입학년도-present>라고 적는 것도 가능하다.

<2018 ~ 현재 협성대학 신학과 재학 중>

Hyupsung University, Hwaseong, Department of Theology**,** 2018-**present**

Hyupsung University, Hwaseong, Department of Theology
2018-**present**

* 보편적으로 이력서에서는 <Department> 앞에 <the>를 생략한다

**** 참고: 학과명**

국문 학과명	영문 학과명
신학과	Department of Theology
사회복지학과	Department of Social Welfare
문예창작학과	Department of Creative Writing
아동보육학과	Department of Child Care & Education
도시개발·행정학과	Department of Urban Development & Administration
미디어영상광고학과	Department of Media and Advertising

경영학과	Management & Information[19]
금융·세무학과	Department of Finance & Insurance, Tax & Accounting
호텔관광·유통경영학과	Hotel & Tourism, Distribution Management
글로벌통상·문화학과 미주통상문화학과	Department of Global Trade and Culture Department of Americas International Trade and Culture
중국어문화학과 중국통상·문화학과	Department of Chinese Language and Literature Department of Chinese Trade and Culture
컴퓨터공학과	Department of Computer Engineering
보건관리학과	Department of Health Management
도시공학과	Department of Urban Planning & Engineering
건축공학과	Department of Architectural Engineering
스마트시스템소프트웨어공학과	Department of Smart Systems Software Engineering
생명과학과	Department of Biological Science
산업디자인학과	Department of Industrial Design
성악·작곡과	Department of Voice and Composition
기악과	Department of Instrumental Music
생활공간디자인학과	Department of Life Space Design
시각조형디자인학과	Visual Formative Arts Design

**** 참고: 학위명**

국문 학위명	영문 학위명
신학사	Bachelor of Theology
문학사	Bachelor of Arts
행정학사	Bachelor of Public Administration
광고홍보미디어학사	Bachelor of Science in Advertising, Public Relations and Media
경영학사	Bachelor of Business Administration
무역학사	Bachelor of International Trade
공학사	Bachelor of Engineering
이학사	Bachelor of Science
디자인학사	Bachelor of Design
음악학사	Bachelor of Music

19) 일반적으로 <경영학과> 영문표기는 <Business Administration>이다.

국문 이력서와 마찬가지로 영문 이력서에서도 처음 직장을 구하는 신입사원인 경우 경력이 부족하기 때문에 인사담당자에게 강하게 어필할 수 있는 경험을 제시하지 않는 한 학력이 가장 중요한 항목으로 작용될 때가 많다. 이와 반대로 경력사원의 경우에는 업무와 직접적으로 관련되는 최근의 경력이 학력보다 더 우선시되므로 최근의 경력에 대해 구체적으로 명시하는 것이 좋다.

최근에 학교를 졸업한 **신입사원**인 경우에는 Header → **Education** → **Work Experience** → Qualifications and Skills → License and Certificate → Activities의 순으로 쓰고, 직장 경험이 있는 **경력사원**인 경우에는 Header → **Work Experience** → **Education** → Qualifications and Skills → License and Certificate → Activities의 순으로 작성한다.

4. Work Experience (경력)

현재 담당하고 있는 업무나 최근에 재직했던 회사의 경력을 기재한다. 경력자인 경우에는 학력보다 경력을 먼저 적는 것이 좋으며 최근의 경력부터 과거로 거슬러가면서 역순으로 자신이 근무했던 회사명, 근무지, 근무기간, 부서 및 직책 그리고 가장 중요하게는 자신이 책임을 지고 담당했던 업무 및 실적에 대해 명시한다. 이때 자신이 수행했던 업무의 성과에 대해 구체적으로 기재함으로써 이를 읽는 상대방으로 하여금 지원자의 능력에 대해 파악할 수 있도록 하는 것이 좋다. 앞에서 언급한 것처럼, 경력은 영문 이력서의 본론이라고 할 만큼 매우 중요한 항목이기 때문에 자신이 부각시키고자 하는 업무 및 성과[20]와 관련된 내용을 Bullet Point[21]를 사용하여 기재하는 것도 좋다.

---

20) '성과'라고 해서 꼭 거창한 내용을 요하는 것이 아니다. 예를 들어 자신이 프로젝트 팀 리더가 아니더라도 주어진 업무를 통해 어떤 것을 배웠고 결과적으로 회사에 기여한 것이 무엇이었는지에 대한 성취도를 감안해서 기재하면 된다.

21) 서류의 중요항목 앞에 네모꼴이나 다이아몬드꼴 또는 원을 붙여 표시하는 것을 말한다:

My shopping lists for this week include:

- Milk
- Yogurt
- Bread
- Eggs

5. Qualifications and Skills (자격 및 특기사항)

외국어나 컴퓨터 능력, 상장 등 인사담당자의 관심을 끌만한 것들 중에서 해당 업무와 관련된 것을 중점적으로 기재한다. 외국어 능력과 관련하여, TOEIC, TOEIC Speaking, TEPS, OPIC 등 구체적인 공인 외국어시험 점수를 적는 것이 좋고 언어구사능력과 관련해서는, 예를 들어 거의 완벽한 경우에는 'fluent'으로 그리고 상대적으로 잘하는 경우에는 'proficient'으로 명시한다. 또한 컴퓨터 활용능력과 관련해서는, 회사에서 주로 사용하는 사무용 프로그램인 Microsoft Office를 기재하는 것이 좋은데, 그 중에서도 업무의 성격상 문서작성이 많은 경우에는 Word로, 발표자료를 만드는 일이 많은 경우에는 PowerPoint로, 그리고 숫자를 분석하는 일이 많은 경우에는 Excel로 기재함으로써 이를 보다 명확하게 적는 것이 좋다.

<사례1>

외국어	영어와 일본어에 능통[22] 토익 925 취득

Foreign Languages: **Fluent in** English and Japanese
Scored 925 **on** the Toeic

<사례2>

컴퓨터	엑셀에 능숙

Computer: **Proficient in (with)** Excel

* ① <**familiar with** the name of the program>은 컴퓨터 활용능력이 완벽하지 않지만 빈번하게 사용하는 어떤 기능에 있어서 익숙한 경우를 말한다.
  ② <**experience with** the name of the program>은 컴퓨터 활용능력이 능숙하지 않을 수 있지만 일부 기능을 사용해본 경험이 있는 경우를 말한다.

<사례3>

올해의 직원상(동메달) 수상, 삼성전자, 2019

Awarded bronze medal for Employee of the year, Samsung Electronics, 2019

22) 외국어 수준을 언급할 때 사용되는 영어단어로는 <fluent>, <proficient>, <intermediate>, <basic> 그리고 <low>가 있다.

6. License and Certificate (면허 및 자격증)

지원자가 소유하고 있는 면허증과 자격증을 간단하게 명시한다. 면허 및 자격증에 대한 정보를 기재하는 정해진 방식은 없지만 각 항목 당 한두 줄로 간단명료하게 적는 것이 바람직하다. 그 과정에서 해당 직무와 관련이 없는 자격증이나 2종 보통 운전면허증과 같이 지극히 평범한 면허증은 별도로 기재하지 않는다.

<사례 1>

2020년 9월 컴퓨터활용능력 1급

Computer Specialist in Spreadsheet & Database Level 1 – September 2020

<사례 2>

2018년 8월 워드프로세서

Word Processor User – August 2018

7. Activities (과외활동)

해외 기업이나 외국계 기업들은 여러 분야에서 다재다능하면서도 적극적인 지원자를 선호한다. 따라서 재학시절에 경험한 다양한 과외활동 예를 들어 실습, 공모전, 봉사활동, 동아리 활동 등을 중심으로 자신이 발휘했던 리더십이나 협동심 및 사회성을 구체적으로 부각시키는 것이 좋다. 작성양식은 활동한 기관의 명칭과 활동기간, 직책 그리고 활동내역을 명시하면 된다. 만약 과외활동이 많은 경우에는 해당 업무와 관련이 있는 활동 경험을 중심으로 3~4개를 선택하여 적는다.

Part 3 영작연습[23)]

다음 이력서를 영작하시오.

1.

황 메리 그레이스 22192 대한민국 인천시 미추홀구 매소홀로 68, 501동 1301호 marygrace@hanmail.net 010-8912-1234

2-1.

학력 2021년 2월 협성대학교 졸업 건축공학(공학사), 컴퓨터공학 부전공 평점: 4.3 성적장학금 받음 (2000년 3월, 2021년 3월)

23) 영문 이력서에 대한 자세한 설명 및 다양한 사례는 다음 영문사이트를 참조할 것을 권한다: https://career.virginia.edu/resumes/creating-your-resume/resume-samples

2-2.

학력	
2021년 2월	협성대학교 졸업
	전공: 건축공학
	부전공: 컴퓨터공학
	평점: 4.3
	성적장학금 받음 (2000년 3월, 2021년 3월)

3.

경력	
2020년 8월 ~ 2021년 2월	DL건설 인천
	인턴, 기술지원부
	기술관리 업무담당

4.

자격 및 특기사항
외국어: 영어에 능통 토익 925점 취득 컴퓨터: Adobe와 Excel에 능숙

5.

면허 및 자격증
2021년 5월 운전면허 1종 보통 2019년 9월 워드프로세서 2017년 10월 유통관리사 2급

6.

과외활동
2019년 6월 ~ 2020년 8월 교환학생으로 밴쿠버 방문 2017년 5월 ~ 2018년 2월 협성대학교 영어동아리 회장

Part 4 정답과 해설

1.

황 메리 그레이스
22192 대한민국 인천시 미추홀구 매소홀로 68, 501동 1301호
marygrace@hanmail.net
010-8912-1234

Mary Grace Hwang
501-1301, 68, Maesohol-ro, Michuhol-gu
Incheon, 22192
Republic of Korea
marygrace@hanmail.net
+82-10-8912-1234

2-1

학력	
2021년 2월	협성대학교 졸업
	건축공학(공학사), 컴퓨터공학 부전공
	평점: 4.3
	성적장학금 받음 (2000년 3월, 2021년 3월)

Education:
Graduated from Hyupsung University, Hwaseong, February 2021
B.E. in Architectural Engineering, minor in Computer Engineering
= Architectural Engineering in Bachelor of Engineering, minor in Computer Engineering
With a GPA 4.3/4.5[24)]
Awarded two scholarships, March 2000 and March 2021

24) 만약 공간의 여유가 충분하지 않을 때에는 평점에 해당하는 내용을 'Engineering' 바로 뒤에 붙여 써도 가능하다: B.E, in Architectural Engineering, minor in Computer Engineering **with a cumulative GPA 4.3/4.5**

2-2

학력
2021년 2월 협성대학교 졸업
전공: 건축공학
부전공: 컴퓨터공학
평점: 4.3
성적장학금 받음 (2000년 3월, 2021년 3월)

Education:

Graduated from Hyupsung University, Hwaseong, February 2021
Major: Architectural Engineering
Minor: Computer Engineering
With a GPA 4.3/4.5
Awarded two scholarships, March 2000 and March 2021

3.

경력
2020년 8월 ~ 2021년 2월 DL건설 인천
인턴, 기술지원부
기술관리 업무담당

Work Experience:

DL Construction, Incheon - August 2020 to February 2021
Intern, Department of Technical Support
Responsibilities include technology management

4.

자격 및 특기사항
외국어: 영어에 능통
토익 925점 취득
컴퓨터: Adobe와 Excel에 능숙

Qualifications and Skills:

Foreign Languages: Fluent in English

Scored 925 on the Toeic

Computer: Proficient in (with) Adobe Software and Excel

5.

면허 및 자격증
2021년 5월 운전면허 1종 보통
2019년 9월 워드프로세서
2017년 10월 유통관리사 2급

License and Certificate:

Driver's License, 1st Class (Ordinary) - May 2021

Word Processor User[25] - September 2019

Distribution Management, Level 2 - October 2017

6.

과외활동
2019년 6월 ~ 2020년 8월 교환학생으로 밴쿠버 방문
2017년 5월 ~ 2018년 2월 협성대학교 영어동아리 회장

Activities:

Exchange student at Vancouver - June 2019 to August 2020

= Attended Vancouver as an exchange student – June 2019 to August 2020

President of the English Club, Hyupsung University - May 2017 to February 2018

25) 현재는 워드프로세서 급수가 단일등급으로 통일됨

Personal History

Mary Grace Hwang

501-1301, 68, Maesohol-ro, Michuhol-gu

Incheon, 22192

Republic of Korea

marygrace@hanmail.net

+82-10-8912-1234

Education

Graduated from Hyupsung University, Hwaseong, February 2021
B.E. in Architectural Engineering, minor in Computer Engineering
With a GPA 4.3/4.5
Awarded two scholarships, March 2000 and March 2021

Work Experience

DL Construction, Incheon - August 2020 to February 2021
Intern, Department of Technical Support
Responsibilities include technology management

Qualifications and Skills

Foreign Languages: Fluent in English
Scored 925 on the Toeic
Computer: Proficient in (with) Adobe Software and Excel

License and Certificate

Driver's License, 1st Class (Ordinary) - May 2021
Word Processor User - September 2019
Distribution Management, Level 2 - October 2017

Activities

Exchange student at Vancouver - June 2019 to August 2020
President of the English Club, Hyupsung University - May 2017 to February 2018

Part 6 Writing Your Personal History

Fundamental Exercises: Rewriting Sentences for the Personal History

다음 이력서 내용을 영작하시오.

1.

학력	2000년 3월 세종고등학교 입학
	2001년 9월 보문고등학교로 전학
	2003년 2월 보문고등학교 졸업

1-1

학력	2015년 3월 협성대학교 입학 2019년 2월 협성대학교 졸업

2.

자격 및 특기사항	토익 850점 취득

3.

자격 및 특기사항	컴퓨터: Adobe와 Excel에 능숙

4.

면허 및 자격증	2010년 10월 운전면허 (1종 대형)

5.

면허 및 자격증	2015년 3월 무역영어 1급 2017년 5월 유통관리사 2급

6.

과외활동	2016년 7월 ~ 2017년 8월 교환학생으로 UCLA 방문

7.

과외활동	2017년 3월 ~ 2018년 2월 캐나다에서 영어연수

6장

영문 비즈니스 레터

비즈니스 레터는 개인의 사적인 편지가 아니라 경제활동과 관련되는 다양한 공식적인 문서이다. 이러한 이유에서 영문 비즈니스 레터를 작성할 때는 내용과 형식에 있어서 보다 많은 주의를 기울여야 한다. 비즈니스 레터는 격식을 갖춘 문체를 바탕으로 당사자가 전달하고자 하는 내용을 간결하면서도 명확하게 전달해야 한다. 긍정적인 어조로 가능한 자신의 감정을 배제한 객관적인 입장에서 서술해야 하며 그 과정에서 자신이 부각시키고자 하는 키워드를 주어 자리에 넣어 표현하는 것이 좋다. 예를 들어 <It is important that this project should be completed by tomorrow.>라는 문장과 <This project should be completed by tomorrow.>라는 문장을 비교해보면, 가주어(It)를 사용한 전자의 경우보다 'This project'를 주어로 사용한 후자의 경우에서 상대방의 시선을 더욱 집중시키고 있음을 알 수 있다. 또한 비즈니스 레터의 문체와 관련하여, 구어적 표현의 비격식체(informal style)보다 격식체(formal style) 영어를 사용하여 문서를 작성할 것을 권한다. 또한 문서를 작성하는 과정에서 흔히 쓰는 <I'm>, <He's>, <It's>와 같은 단축형 표현보다는 이것을 <I am>, <He is>, <It is>로 바꾸어 표현하는 것이 좋으며 구어, 유행어, 약어, 속어는 사용하지 않는 것을 추천한다.

Part 1 Basic Business Letter Rules (5 C's Rules - C로 시작하는 다섯 가지 원칙)

1. Clearness (명확성)

비즈니스 문서는 명확한 의사소통을 근간으로 문서작성자의 의도대로 상대방을 설득시켜야 하기 때문에 자신이 전달하고자 하는 요지가 분명하게 드러나도록 작성되어야 한다. 내용이 명확하지 않으면 이후 분쟁의 소지가 될 수 있기 때문에 어떤 내용의 문서를 쓸지 미리 정리해 둘 필요가 있고, 정확한 단어는 물론 구두점까지도 주의를 기울여서 작성해야 한다. 너무 긴 문장은 바람직하지 않으며 적당한 길이의 내용을 명확하게 표현하는 것이 중요하다. 이때 간과해서 안 될 것은 문단의 구분이다. <하나의 내용은 하나의 단락>이라는 원칙을 가지고 각 단락마다 작성자가 전하고자 하는 내용이 표현되도록 문장을 작성해야 한다. 또한 단락과 단락 사이에는 보통 한 줄을 띄우는데 이것도 명확성을 높이기 위한 일환이다.

example: 내용에 있어서의 명확성

I will ship your order shortly. (X)
→ I will ship your order by March 5. (O)

another example: 구두점(comma)에 있어서의 명확성

If you drive buses it would be a Driver's License 1st Class (Large). (X)
→ If you drive buses, it would be a Driver's License, 1st Class (Large). (O)

2. Conciseness (간결성)

비즈니스 문서는 간단명료하게 작성해야 하는 간결성이 요구된다. 제한된 시간 내에 일을 처리해야 하는 직장인들을 대상으로 하기 때문에 불필요한 내용을 최대한 줄이고 상대방으로 하여금 신속하고도 정확하게 내용을 파악할 수 있도록 간결하게 작성한다. 어구(phrase) 역시 되도록 간단하게 표현하는 것이 좋고 상대방에게 보내는 핵심적인 내용만 요령있게 전달한다.

examples:

a) <a number of>를 <many>로 수정한다.
I received a number of resumes from applicants looking for their jobs yesterday. (△)
→ I received **many** resumes from **job applicants** yesterday. (O)

b) <there is>, <it is>의 사용을 피한다.
In our building, there are five elevators. (△)
→ **Our building has five elevators.** (O)

c) <수동태 문장>을 <능동태 문장>으로 고친다.
Another meeting will be held by Tom tomorrow. (△)
→ **Tom will hold another meeting tomorrow.** (O)

d) 절(clause)보다는 구(phrase), 구보다는 단어(words)를 사용한다.
The enterprise **that is most popular at the present time** is Samsung. (△)
→ The enterprise **most popular at present**[26)]**is Samsung.** (O)
→ **The most popular enterprise at the present time** is Samsung. (OO)

3. Completeness (완전성)

비즈니스 문서는 상대방에게 전하고자 하는 사항을 빠짐없이 담고 있어야 한다. 따라서 문서를 작성한 후에도 자신이 쓰고자 했던 내용이 모두 들어가 있는지 거듭 확인해야 한다. 누락된 내용이 있는 경우에는 추신(P.S.- postscript)을 써서 누락된 내용을 보완하기보다 처음부터 문서를 다시 작성해야 한다.

4. Courtesy (정중성)

비즈니스 문서는 예의를 갖추어 상대방을 설득하거나 이해시키는 어조로 작성되어야 한다. 이때 지나친 미사여구나 성의가 느껴지지 않는 '겉치레 말' 은 상대방에게 오히려 불신감을 줄 수 있기 때문에 이를 사용하지 않는 것이 좋으며, 가급적 작성자(I)가 아닌 상대방(You)의 입장에서 문서를 작성할 것을 권장한다.

---

26) 형용사에 수식어구가 결합된 경우에는 명사 뒤에서 후치수식한다. 참고로 comma rule(쉼표규칙)과 관련하여, most 앞과 present 뒤에 쉼표를 붙이는 것은 본인의 선택사항이다.

examples:

a) **I → You** (상대방 위주로 'You'를 활용한다.)
I appreciate your order.
→ **Your order** is very appreciated. (O)

b) **must → have to** (완곡표현-더 부드러운 표현)
You must visit the branch office.
→ You **have to** visit the branch office. (O)

c) **will → would** (더 공손한 표현)
Will you send me the report?
→ **Would** you send me the report? (O)

5. Correctness (정확성)

비즈니스 문서는 내용의 정확성뿐만 아니라 문법, 철자, 구두점, 심지어 숫자 쓰는 방법에 이르기까지 모든 형식에 있어서도 정확하게 작성되어야 한다.

examples:

The project was finished, while working with him. (X)
(주절에서 분사구문의 주어, 다시 말해 그와 함께 일한 주체가 없다.)
→ **We** finished the project while working with him. (O)
= While working with him**, we** finished the project.

To improve your ability in English, practice is needed. (X)
(주절에 영어능력을 향상시키는 주체가 없다)
→ To improve your ability in English, **you** have to practice. (O)

The president know where the fax is. (X)
(주어와 동사의 수일치: 주어가 3인칭 단수일 때 동사 역시 단수동사가 되어야 한다)
→ The president **knows** where the fax is. (O)

The meeting will be at 12:00. (X)
(언급하고자 하는 시간이 정오인지 자정인지 정확하게 기재되어야 한다.)
→ The meeting will be **at noon.** (O)

Part 2 General Outline of a Business Letter in English

First Name Last Name
Sender's Address
(additional contact info, such as email, phone number, etc)

Recipient's Name
Title - 선택사항
Company
Recipient's Address
Recipient's City, State/Province, Postal code

Date

Dear Mr/Mrs/Ms ··· (If you are unsure of using Mrs, then use Ms.) If you cannot determine gender (for Mr/Mrs/Ms), then you can use the full name, like Dear Alex Park.

Introduction paragraph. Here you would introduce yourself, or the reason for your letter. You will want to be polite but concise, and briefly have a main point.

Body paragraphs. The body of the letter should discuss the main point. This should be 2 or 3 paragraphs, and not much longer. Your letter should fit on one page. The information presented here, should justify the main point. You can also include background information and details that would support your point.

When formatting this letter, the paragraphs should be justified to the left, and have one blank space between paragraphs. The paragraphs should also be single-spaced. This format is standard in business writing, and is called **block format**. You can show a small amount of creativity in the header.

In the **header**, you can increase the font sizes, change the font entirely, or change the alignment to something other than left alignment. Keep in mind of who will be reading your letter. If the recipient of the letter is from a very conservative company, then you will want to keep your creativity level on the lower end. To make your letter stand out, you can also add colour to your header.

We are now nearing the end of the page, and you will insert your **conclusion** here, or **closing paragraph**. This should only be a few sentences. Below will be the formal closing. You will want to leave space for your written signature (unless this is being sent by email). If being mailed, you will also enclose the word, **Enclosure** when you are mailing accompanying documents (such as a resume) with this letter.

Sincerely,

Signature
Sender's Name

Enclosure

⬇

<해설>

First Name Last Name (발신자의 이름 성)
Sender's Address (발신자 주소: 번지, 동, 구, 시, 우편번호, 국가)
(additional contact info, such as email, phone number, etc) (추가연락처)

Recipient's Name (수신자 이름)
Title (제목)[27)]
Company (회사명)
Recipient's Address (수신자 주소)
Recipient's City, State/Province, Postal code (우편번호)

Date (발신 날짜)

Dear Mr/Mrs/Ms (인사말: 서론인사 및 호칭)··· (If you are unsure of using Mrs, then use Ms.) If you cannot determine gender (for Mr/Mrs/Ms), then you can use the full name(완전한 이름), like Dear Alex Park.

Introduction (서론). Here you would introduce yourself, or the reason for your letter. You will want to be polite but concise, and have a main point(요점, 주제)
→ 간단한 자기소개와 더불어 본문내용의 개략적인 내용을 적는다

Body of letter (본문 - 본론). The body of the letter should discuss the main point. This should be 2 or 3 paragraphs, and not much longer. Your letter should fit on(잘 맞다) one page. The information presented here, should justify(보여주다) the main point. You can also include background information and details that would support(뒷받침하다) your point.

27) 비즈니스 문서의 제목표기는 선택사항이다.

When formatting this letter, the paragraphs should be justified to the left(왼쪽 정렬), and have one blank space (한 줄 띄우기) between paragraphs. The paragraphs should also be single-spaced (기본 줄간격).[28] This format is standard in business writing(비즈니스 글쓰기), and is called **block format.** You can show a small amount of creativity in the header(= letterhead: 발신자 이름과 주소 적는 란)

In the **header**, you can increase the font sizes(글자크기), change the font(글의 모양-서체) entirely, or change the alignment to something other than(~가 아닌) left alignment. Keep in mind(명심하다) of who will be reading your letter. If the recipient of the letter is from a very conservative company, then you will want to keep your creativity(독창성) level(정도) on the lower end(낮은 단계에서의). To make your letter stand out(부각시키다), you can also add colour to your header.

We are now nearing(가까워지다) the end of the page, and you will insert your **conclusion**(결론) here, or closing paragraph(마지막 단락). This should only be a few sentences. Below will be the formal closing(끝인사). You will want to leave space for your written signature (unless this is being sent by email). If being mailed, you will also enclose(덧붙인다) the word, **Enclosure,** when you are mailing accompanying documents(함께 보내는 서류) (such as a resume) with this letter.

Sincerely (끝인사),

Signature (서명: 서명할 곳에 선을 그을 필요는 없다)

Sender's Name (발신자 이름)

Enclosure

28) single-space 설명: Single-spacing the lines in a paragraph means you have no spaces between the lines in the entire paragraph. But if you say to leave one single (blank or empty) space between the paragraphs, then that means to leave one empty space there. I think the key words are "blank" or "empty".

Part 3 How to Write a Business Letter

1. Header (= Letterhead): 발신자 이름과 주소 및 연락처 적는 난

누가 쓴 편지인가를 표시하기 위한 것으로 편지지 머리부문에 발신자의 회사이름, 주소, 전화번호 및 이메일 주소 등을 적는다.

① First Name Last Name (이름 성)
② Sender's Address (발신자 주소: 번지, 동, 구, 시, 우편번호, 국가[29])
(additional contact info, such as email, phone number, etc)
(추가연락처 – 메일주소, 전화번호, 팩스번호 등)

header는 경우에 따라 어느 정도 독창적으로 작성할 수 있다. 예를 들어 글자크기를 키운다든지, 글자의 모양을 바꾸거나 왼쪽 정렬이 아닌 다른 정렬로 변경할 수 있으며 나아가 글자를 컬러로 입힐 수도 있다.

2. Recipient's Address (수신자 이름과 주소)[30]

비즈니스 레터를 받는 수신자의 이름, 회사명, 주소를 적는다. 일반적으로 첫째 줄에 수신자의 이름을 쓰고, 다음 줄에 회사명을 쓴 후 줄을 바꿔서 그 다음 줄에 주소를 쓰는데 국제우편인 경우 국가명은 마지막 행에 독립해서 쓴다.

Mr. Edward A. Martins
New York Trading Co., LTD.
250 Fifth Avenue
New York NY, 10042-0355
U.S.A.

29) 국제우편인 경우 국가명을 기재한다.

30) 일반적으로 header 밑으로 두 줄 아래에 기재하는 경향을 보이지만, 쓰고자 하는 편지내용의 전체 길이를 참작하여 적당히 조정한다.

3. Date (발신 일자)[31]

비즈니스 편지에서 날짜는 중요한 의미를 갖는다. 어떤 문제가 발생하였을 때 상대방에게 <언제 전달했는가>가 쟁점이 되거나 해결의 실마리가 되기 때문이다. 발신 일자는 정확히 기재되어야 하며 비즈니스 문서에서 날짜가 없는 것은 무효라고 해도 과언이 아니다.

① 날짜 쓰는 법: 월 일, 년도 (May 2, 2001)
② 달(month)을 표기할 때 Aug, Sept, Oct와 같이 약어로 기재하지 말고, 날짜를 기입할 때도 숫자만으로 표기하지 않는다. 예를 들면 2001년 5월 2일을 5/2/01과 같이 적는 것이 그러한 사례이다.

4. Salutation (인사말)[32]: 서론 인사 및 호칭

수신자의 성별을 모르는 경우	full name	Dear. Alex Park:
수신자 이름과 직함을 모르는 경우	1인 남성 1인 여성	Dear Sir: Dear Ms: / Dear Madam:
수신자 이름만 알고 있는 경우 수신자 직함만 알고 있는 경우	상대가 1인	Dear Mr. Brown: Dear Hiring Manager:
수신자 이름과 직함 그리고 성별을 모르는 경우		To Whom It May Concern:[33]

**** 참고**

경칭 뒤에 붙은 colon(:)은 콤마(,)보다 더 정중한 표현으로 간주되기 때문에 격식을 갖추어야 하는 비즈니스 레터를 작성할 때 가급적 colon을 사용하는 것이 바람직하다.

Dear Sir**:** (격식체)
Dear Sir**,** (비격식체)

**** 참고**

발신자와 수신자가 서로 잘 아는 관계에서는 'Dear'나 'Hello (Hi)' 다음에 이름을 쓰고 쉼표를 붙여도 된다:

Dear Ruth,
Hi Ruth,

---

31) 일반적으로 수신자의 주소 밑으로 두 줄 아래 기재하는 경향을 보이지만, 쓰고자 하는 편지내용의 전체 길이를 참작하여 적당히 조정한다.

32) 일반적으로 발신일자 밑으로 두 줄 아래에 기재하는 경향을 보이지만, 쓰고자 하는 편지내용의 전체 길이를 참작하여 적당히 조정한다.

33) 단어의 첫 글자를 모두 대문자로 표기한다.

5. Introduction (서론)[34] (도입부)

간단한 자기소개와 더불어 편지 본론의 개략적인 내용을 간단하게 요점만 적는다.

6. Body of letter (본문)[35]

본문은 서신에 있어 발신자의 의사를 상대방에게 전달하는 데 가장 중요한 부분이다. 무엇을 전달하고 무엇을 생략할 것인지 그리고 전달해야 할 사항을 어떻게 표현할 것인가에 대해 구체적으로 생각하는 것이 중요하며 요점을 뒷받침할 수 있는 세부사항이나 배경 정보도 포함할 수 있어야 한다. 왼쪽 정렬을 기준으로 단락과 단락 사이에는 한 줄을 띄우고, 기본 줄간격을 유지하면서 분량은 3~4개의 단락으로 구성하는 것이 바람직하다. 결론에서는 결론에 해당되는 내용과 더불어 길지 않은 2~3줄의 내용이 적당하다.

7. Closing (끝인사)

본론을 끝낸 후에 인사처럼 쓰는 말이다. 특별한 뜻은 없고 '감사합니다' 정도로 보면 된다.

일반적인 비즈니스 서신	Sincerely, Sincerely yours, Yours sincerely,
격식을 차려야 하는 공식적인 비즈니스 서신	Truly yours, Yours truly,
정부관료나 대학교수에게 보내는 비즈니스 서신	Respectfully, Respectfully yours, Yours respectfully,
친분이 있는 직장 동료나 부하직원에게 보내는 비즈니스 서신	Best regards,[36] Regards, Best wishes,[37]

끝인사 아래에는 (e-mail이 아닌 경우) 자필서명을 할 수 있는 공간을 남기는 것이 좋다.

34) 일반적으로 인사말 밑으로 한 줄 아래에 기재하는 경향을 보이지만, 쓰고자 하는 편지내용의 전체 길이를 참작하여 적당히 조정한다.

35) 서론 밑으로 한 줄 아래에서 시작한다.

36) 'Best regards'에서 'regards'의 첫 글자(r)는 소문자로 기재한다.

37) 'Best wishes'에서 'wishes'의 첫 글자(w)는 소문자로 기재한다.

8. Enclosure (동봉물)[38)]

동봉물이 있는 경우에는 맨 아래에 Enclosure라는 단어를 기입한다. 이때 Enclosure 다음에 colon(:)를 붙이고 동봉하는 문서의 제목 혹은 문서의 개수를 쓴다.

① 동봉문서가 1개인 경우:

Enclosure: Resume

Enclosure: 1

② 동봉문서가 2개 이상인 경우:

Enclosures: Resume, Application Form

Enclosures: 2

38) 일반적으로 수신자의 이름 밑으로 네 줄 아래에 기재하는 경향을 보이지만, 쓰고자 하는 편지내용의 전체 길이를 참작하여 적당히 조정한다.

Part 4 Example of a Properly Formatted Business Letter: Recommendation Letter

추천서

김민수
상명대학교 영어과
03016 대한민국 서울 종로구 홍지문 2길 20
대한민국
kim-thomas@hanmail.net
010-6621-1234

Mr. Edward Martins, Hiring Manager
Vancouver Trading Co., LTD
1234 Highway Road
Vancouver BC, V1V 1V1
Canada

2022년 3월 15일

담당자 귀하

저는 한국 서울 소재 상명대학교 영어과 소속 김민수 교수입니다. 박민숙을 귀사의 사장 비서직으로 추천하게 되어 매우 기쁩니다. 그녀의 대학원 지도교수로서, 저는 2015년에서 2018년까지 그녀의 학위논문을 지도했고, 그녀는 우리 학교에 있었던 최고의 학생들 가운데 한 학생이었습니다.

저는 그녀의 열심히 일하는 태도, 진취성, 그리고 언어, 특히 영어와 불어의 유창함 때문에 그녀의 연구를 지도하는 것을 무척이나 즐길 수 있었습니다. 특히 그녀의 영어에 있어서의 읽기, 말하기, 그리고 쓰기 능력은 영어를 모국어로 하는 사람의 것과 거의 동일하다고 확신합니다. 또한, 그녀는 타자를 빨리 치며 엑셀, 파워포인트, 그리고 워드와 같은 모든 소프트웨어 프로그램에 매우 능숙합니다.

저는 박민숙을 비서로서 유럽국가에서 온 많은 바이어들과 국제무역을 거래하는 귀사에 강력히 추천합니다. 저는 그녀가 그녀의 뛰어난 언어능력과 사교성을 가지고 어떤 비서업무도 처리할 수 있을 것이라고 확신합니다. 저는 당신이 그녀에게 이 일자리를 주는 것을 후회하지 않을 것이라고 확신합니다. 그녀의 자격과 관련하여 질문이 있으시면 +82-10-6621-1234로 연락하시거나 메일로 편하게 연락주십시요.

김민수

김민수 교수
상명대학교 영어과

<English Words and Idioms>

recommendation letter 추천서
Department of English 영어과

Prof. 교수 professor 약어
recommend someone for ~를 ~에 추천하다
secretary position of the president 사장 비서직
academic adviser 지도교수
graduate school 대학원
supervise 지도하다
dissertation 학위논문

hard-working attitude 열심히 일하는 태도
enterprising spirit 진취성
proficiency in ~의 유창함 / ~의 능숙함
guide 지도하다
research work 연구
sure 확신하는
skill 능력
the same as ~과 동일하게
native English speaker 영어를 모국어로 사용하는 사람 (영어가 모국어인 사람)
proficient in ~에 능숙한
such as ~과 같은

firm 회사
deal in ~을 거래하다
European countries 유럽국가
positive 확신하는
cope with 처리하다
secretarial duties 비서업무
excellent 뛰어난
language skill 언어능력
sociability 사교성
regret ~ing ~을 후회하다
position 일자리 (직업)
get in touch with 와 연락하다
regarding ~과 관련하여
qualification 자격

Part 5 영작연습

다음 문장을 영작하시오.

추천서

→ ____________

김민수

→ ____________

상명대학교 영어과

→ ______________________________

03016 대한민국 서울 종로구 홍지문 2길 20

→____

kim-thomas@hanmail.net

010-6621-1234

→ _________________________

____

2022년 3월 15일

→ ________________________

담당자 귀하

→ ________________________

1. The First Paragraph

저는 한국 서울 소재 상명대학교 영어과 소속 김민수 교수입니다.

→ ____

<Prof. / Department of English / from / at>

박민숙을 귀사의 사장 비서직으로 추천하게 되어 매우 기쁩니다.

→ ____

<my great pleasure / recommend someone for>

그녀의 대학원 지도교수로서, 저는 2015년에서 2018년까지 그녀의 학위논문을 지도했고, 그녀는 우리 학교에 있었던 최고의 학생들 가운데 한 학생이었습니다.

→ ____

____

<academic adviser / supervise / dissertation / that I have had at my school>

2. The Second Paragraph

저는 그녀의 열심히 일하는 태도, 진취성, 그리고 언어, 특히 영어와 불어의 유창함 때문에 그녀의 연구를 지도하는 것을 무척이나 즐길 수 있었습니다.

→ ____

____

<highly enjoy / research work / hard-working attitude / enterprising spirit / her proficiency in>

특히 그녀의 영어에 있어서의 읽기, 말하기, 그리고 쓰기 능력은 영어를 모국어로 하는 사람의 것과 거의 동일하다고 확신합니다.

→ ____

____

<sure / skills in English / the same as / native English speakers'>

또한, 그녀는 타자를 빨리 치며 엑셀, 파워포인트, 그리고 워드와 같은 모든 소프트웨어 프로그램에 매우 능숙합니다.

→ ____

____

<also / quick typist / proficient in / such as>

3. The Third Paragraph

저는 박민숙을 비서로서 유럽국가에서 온 많은 바이어들과 국제무역을 거래하는 귀사에 강력히 추천합니다.

→ ____

____

<strongly / your firm / which / deal in / European countries>

저는 그녀가 그녀의 뛰어난 언어능력과 사교성을 가지고 어떤 비서업무도 처리할 수 있을 것이라고 확신합니다.

→ ____

____

<very positive / that / cope with / secretarial duties / excellent / sociability>

저는 당신이 그녀에게 이 일자리를 주는 것을 후회하지 않을 것이라고 확신합니다.

→ ____

<feel sure / regret ~ing / position>

그녀의 자격과 관련하여 질문이 있으시면 +82-10-6621-1234로 연락하시거나 메일로 편하게 연락주십시요.

→ ____

____

<feel free / get in touch with / at / by / regarding / qualification>

김민수

김민수 교수
상명대학교 영어과

→ ______________________________

____

____

Part 6 정답과 해설

추천서

→ Recommendation Letter

김민수

→ Minsu Kim

상명대학교 영어과

→ Department of English, Sangmyung University

03016 대한민국 서울 종로구 홍지문 2길 20

→ 20, Hongjimun 2-gil, Jongno-gu

Seoul, 03016

Republic of Korea

kim-thomas@hanmail.net

010-6621-1234

→ kim-thomas@hanmail.net

+82–10–6621-1234

2022년 3월 15일

→ March 15, 2022

담당자 귀하

→ To Whom It May Concern:

1. The First Paragraph:

추천서 서론에서는 지원자와의 관계 및 지원자와 얼마 동안 함께 일을 했는지에 대해 언급한다.

저는 한국 서울 소재 상명대학교 영어과 소속 김민수 교수입니다.

<Prof. / Department of English / from / at>

→ I am Prof. Minsu Kim from the Department of English at Sangmyung University in Seoul, Korea.

박민숙을 귀사의 사장 비서직으로 추천하게 되어 매우 기쁩니다.

<my great pleasure / recommend someone for>

→ It is my great pleasure to recommend Minsook Park for the secretary position of the president at your company.

= It is my great pleasure **and privilege to highly** recommend Minsook Park for '**the secretary to the president**' **position** at your company.

그녀의 대학원 지도교수로서, 저는 2015년에서 2018년까지 그녀의 학위논문을 지도했고, 그녀는 우리 학교에 있었던 최고의 학생들 가운데 한 학생이었습니다.

<academic adviser / supervise / dissertation / that I have had at my school>

→ As her academic adviser at the graduate school, I supervised her dissertation from 2015 to 2018 and she was one of my best students that I have had at my school.

= As her academic adviser at the graduate school, I supervised **Ms. Park's** dissertation from 2015 to 2018. **She proved to be** one of my best students that I have had **the pleasure to work with.**

2. The Second Paragraph:

본론에서는 지원자를 추천하는 이유, 구체적으로 지원자의 강점이나 특기 및 자질에 대해 언급한다.

저는 그녀의 열심히 일하는 태도, 진취성, 그리고 언어, 특히 영어와 불어의 유창함 때문에 그녀의 연구를 지도하는 것을 무척이나 즐길 수 있었습니다.

<highly enjoy / research work / hard-working attitude / enterprising spirit / her proficiency in>

→ I could highly enjoy guiding her research work because of her hard-working attitude, enterprising spirit, and her proficiency in languages, especially English and French.

= **Not only was she always full of energy, but she was also consistent in displaying a very positive attitude, and an enterprising spirit. Ms. Park is proficient** in English and French.

특히 그녀의 영어에 있어서의 읽기, 말하기, 그리고 쓰기 능력은 영어를 모국어로 하는 사람의 것과 거의 동일하다고 확신합니다.

<sure / skills in English / the same as / native English speakers'>

→ I am sure that especially, her reading, speaking, and writing skills in English are almost the same as the native English speakers'.

= **Her comprehension, speaking, and writing skills in English are comparable to a** native English **speaker' .**

또한, 그녀는 타자를 빨리 치며 엑셀, 파워포인트, 그리고 워드와 같은 모든 소프트웨어 프로그램에 매우 능숙합니다.

<also / quick typist / proficient in / such as>

→ Also, she is a quick typist and very proficient in all the software programs such as Excel, PowerPoint and Word.

= **In addition,** she is a quick typist and very **knowledgeable of** all the **softwares used at the Department of English at Sangmyung University.**

3. The Third Paragraph:

결론에서는 지원자를 강력하게 추천한다는 것을 다시 강조하면서 담당자가 연락할 수 있는 연락처를 남기는 것이 좋다.

저는 박민숙을 비서로서 유럽국가에서 온 많은 바이어들과 국제무역을 거래하는 귀사에 강력히 추천합니다.

<strongly / your firm / which / deal in / European countries>

→ I strongly recommend Minsook Park as a secretary **for** your firm, which has dealt in international trade with many buyers from European countries.

* 위 문장에서 전치사 for 대신에 to를 사용해도 올바른 문장이다. 영국에서는 <recommend A for B>라는 구문을 올바른 표현으로 간주하고, 북미에서는 <recommend A to B>라는 구문을 올바른 표현으로 간주하는, 각각의 차이를 보인다. 따라서 위 문맥에서 전치사 to를 사용해도 올바른 문장이다.

= I strongly recommend Minsook Park as a secretary **to** your firm, which has dealt in international trade with many buyers from European countries.

= **I am very confident that Minsook Park will be an important asset to your business, specially in international trade and dealing with foreign buyers.**

저는 그녀가 그녀의 뛰어난 언어능력과 사교성을 가지고 어떤 비서업무도 처리할 수 있을 것이라고 확신합니다.

<very positive / that / cope with / secretarial duties / excellent / sociability>

→ I am very positive that she will be able to cope with any secretarial duties with her excellent language skills and her sociability.

저는 당신이 그녀에게 이 일자리를 주는 것을 후회하지 않을 것이라고 확신합니다.

<feel sure / regret ~ing / position>

→ I feel sure that you will not regret giving her this position.

그녀의 자격과 관련하여 질문이 있으시면 +82-10-6621-1234로 연락하시거나 메일로 편하게 연락주십시요.

<feel free / get in touch with / at / by / regarding / qualification>

→ Please feel free to get in touch with me at +82-10-6621-1234 or by an email if you have any questions regarding her qualifications.

= **Should you need further information, please do not hesitate to** get in touch with me at +82-10-6621-1234 or by an email.

Sincerely,

끝인사와 더불어 자신의 이름, 직책 및 소속 기관 등에 대해 언급한다.

김민수

김민수 교수

상명대학교 영어과

→ Minsu Kim, Professor
Department of English
Sangmyung University

Recommendation Letter

Minsu Kim
Department of English, Sangmyung University
20, Hongjimun 2-gil, Jongno-gu
Seoul, 03016
Republic of Korea
kim-thomas@hanmail.net
+82-10-6621-1234

Mr. Edward Martins, Hiring Manager
Vancouver Trading Co., LTD
1234 Highway Road
Vancouver BC, V1V 1V1
Canada

March 15, 2022

To Whom It May Concern:

I am Prof. Minsu Kim from the Department of English at Sangmyung University in Seoul, Korea. It is my great pleasure to recommend Minsook Park for the secretary position of the president at your company. As her academic adviser at the graduate school, I supervised her dissertation from 2015 to 2018 and she was one of my best students that I have had at my school.

I could highly enjoy guiding her research work because of her hard-working attitude, enterprising spirit, and her proficiency in languages, especially English and French. I am sure that especially, her reading, speaking, and writing skills in English are almost the same as the native English speakers'. Also, she is a quick typist and very proficient in all the software programs such as Excel, PowerPoint, and Word.

I strongly recommend Minsook Park as a secretary to your firm, which has dealt in international trade with many buyers from European countries. I am very positive that she will be able to cope with any secretarial duties with her excellent language skills and her sociability. I feel sure that you will not regret giving her this position. Please feel free to get in touch with me at +82-10-6621-1234 or by an email if you have any questions regarding her qualifications.

Sincerely,

Minsu Kim

Minsu Kim, Professor
Department of English
Sangmyung University

Recommendation Letter

Minsu Kim
Department of English, Sangmyung University
20, Hongjimun 2-gil, Jongno-gu,
Seoul, 03016
Republic of Korea
kim-thomas@hanmail.net
+82-10-6621-1234

Mr. Edward Martins, Hiring Manager
Vancouver Trading Co., LTD
1234 Highway Road
Vancouver BC, V1V 1V1
Canada

March 15, 2022

To Whom It May Concern:

It is my great pleasure and privilege to highly recommend Minsook Park for 'the secretary to the president' position at your company.

As her academic adviser at the graduate school, I supervised Ms. Park dissertation from 2015 to 2018. She proved to be one of my best students that I have had the pleasure to work with. Not only was she always full of energy, but she was also consistent in displaying a very positive attitude, and an enterprising spirit.

Ms. Park is proficient in English and French. Her comprehension, writing and speaking skills in English are comparable to the native English speakers'. In addition, she is a quick typist and very knowledgeable of all the softwares used at the Department of English at Sangmyung University.

I am very confident that Minsook Park will be an important asset to your firm. Her secretarial skills, command of several languages, contagious positive attitude toward hard-work and pleasing personality, I feel will greatly assist in your business, specially in international trade and dealing with foreign buyers.

Should you need further information, please do not hesitate to get in touch with me at +82-10-6621-1234 or by an email.

Sincerely,

Minsu Kim

Minsu Kim, Professor
Department of English
Sangmyung University

Fundamental Exercises

* 비즈니스 레터 작성 시 주의해야 할 다섯 가지 C의 법칙들이 있다. 다음 문장의 수정과정을 보고 적용된 C의 법칙을 적으시오. (1~2)

1. You have to submit your job application soon

   → You have to submit your job application by Friday.

→ ______________________________

2. In our building, there are five elevators.

   → Our building has five elevators.

→ ______________________________

3. 비즈니스 레터에서 발신일자(date)가 들어가야 할 곳은 어디인가?

   ① header 밑에　② recipient's address 밑에　③ introduction 위에　④ closing 위에

4. 다음 문장을 읽고 밑줄 친 부분에 적합한 단어들을 고르시오.

It is my great pleasure to ________ Minsook Park _______ the secretary position of the presidnet at your company. (박민숙을 귀사의 사장 비서직으로 추천하게 되어 매우 기쁩니다.)

   ① recommendation, toward
   ② recommend, for
   ③ recommend, into
   ④ recommendable, within

5. 비즈니스 레터 형식과 관련하여, 다음 내용을 읽고 괄호 안에 들어갈 적합한 단어를 적으시오.

When formatting business letters, the paragraphs should be justified to the left, and have one blank space between paragraphs. The paragraphs should also be single-spaced. This format is standard in business writing, and is called __________.

→ ______________________________

7장

비즈니스 레터 작성시 유의사항과 자기소개법

Part 1 비지니스 레터 작성 시 유의사항

1. 호칭

한국에서는 김 부장님, 박 과장님과 같이 성 다음에 직책이나 직급을 붙여서 상대방을 호칭한다. 그러나 영어권 국가에서는 직급 다음에 성을 붙여 상대방을 부른다:

Example: President Kim (O)
Kim President (X)

<직급명칭>

사장	President
부사장	Vice President
전무	Executive Director
상무	Managing Director
이사	Director
부장	General Manager
차장	Senior Manager
과장	Manager
대리	Assistant Manager
직원	Employee - representative, staff

<회사 부서명>

이하 부서명과 관련해서, △ 표시를 한 것은 비공식적으로 통용되는 용어를 의미하고 완전히 틀린 표현인 경우에는 X 표시를 하였다.

사장실

office of the President, CEO

비서실

office of the secretary

기획부 (기획실)

department of planning
= planning department
= planning (△)

연구개발부

department of research and development
= research and development department
= research and development (△)

인사부 (인력개발부)

department of human resources
= human resources department (= personnel department)
= human resources (△)

기술지원부

department of technical support
= technical support department
= technical support (△)

총무부

department of administration
= administration department
= general administration
≠ general affairs department (X)

홍보부

department of public relations
= public relations department
= public relations (△)

마케팅부

department of marketing
= marketing department
= finance (△)
≠ financial (X)

회계부 (경리부)[39]

department of accounting
= accounting department
= accounting (△)

영업관리부

department of sales administration
= sales administration department
= sales administration (△)

자재부

department of materials
= materials department
≠ materials (X)

구매부

department of purchasing
= purchasing department
= purchasing (△)

---

39)회계부와 재무부의 차이: **Finance and Accounting are slightly different, but also the same.** The **<accounting department>** includes billing customers, preparing financial statements, payroll, paying the business bills, etc,. The **<finance department>** includes the above, but also is about acquiring funds for the business (investments) and planning for those funds (investment planning and reporting to investors). In larger companies, "accounting" is part of the Finance Department. **In smaller companies,** it is usually just referred to as **the Accounting Department** (there would be no Finance department).

생산부

production department (O)
= department of production (X)
≠ production (X)

생산관리부

department of production control
= production control department
= production control (△)

품질관리부

department of quality control
= quality control department
= quality control (△)

고객지원부

department of customer support
= customer support department
= customer support (△)

물류부

department of logistics
= logistics department
= logistics (△)

국내영업부

department of domestic sales
= domestic sales department
= domestic sales and marketing (△)

해외영업부

department of overseas sales
= overseas sales department
= overseas sales (△)
= overseas sales and marketing (△)

department of international sales
= international sales department
= international sales (△)
= international sales and marketing (△)

해외사업부

department of overseas operations
= overseas operations department
= overseas operations (△)

department of international operations
= international operations department
= international operations (△)

** 참고: 부서명을 대문자로 쓰는 경우와 그렇지 않은 경우:[40)]

If you are using the name of a general department, then do not capitalize it. If you are using it **as a proper noun**, then it would be **capitalized**, that is, the names of departments are **capitalized only when using the full, formal name**.

Examples:

① I worked in **Continuing Studies** at SFU, supporting various languages programs.
② **The human resources departments** at the universities would have information about the hiring practices of their academic departments.
③ **The research and development department** at Samsung must have some very talented people working for them.

Therefore, please try to find the full, formal names of departments on the company website or other social media. For example, with regard to HR, you need to find out if the full, formal name is "Department of Human Resources" or if it is "Human Resources Department", which can be problematic if you do not have that information available. Sometimes, in smaller companies, "Human Resources Department" or "Department of Human Resources" can be interchangeable.

40) 부서명과 관련하여 대문자 쓰는 규칙에 대한 내용은 다음 영문사이트를 참조할 것을 권한다:
https://www.rochester.edu/news/styleguide/capitals.html
https://www.cu.edu/university-relations/capitalization

Examples:

① Lisa is a professor from the **Department of English**. (formal name)

Lisa is a professor from the **English department**. (informal name).

② If a company's formal department name for HR is the **Department of Hurman Resources**[41]:

- Gordon is a manager in the **Department of Human Resources**. (formal name)
- Gordon is a manager in the **human resources department**. (informal name)
- Gordon is a manger with **human resources.** (informal)
- Gordon is a manger in **human resources**. (informal)

2. 공식문서에서 자신의 이름을 소개할 때

자신의 이름(first name)과 성(last name)을 기재한다: <My name is David Kim.>, <I am David Kim.>, <This is David Kim.>

* 자신을 소개할 때 <I am .. >과 <This is .. > 둘 다 사용할 수 있다. 이것은 개인의 선호에 따른 선택사항이지만, 일반적으로 수신자가 발신자 혹은 발신자의 회사에 대해 이미 알고 있는 상황에서는 <This is>를 쓰고 그렇지 않은 경우에는 <I am ...>을 쓴다.

3. Its와 It's의 차이

미국인들도 매우 빈번하게 틀리는 부분으로서 잘못 사용되는 경우가 많다. It's는 It is의 줄임말이고 its는 '그것의'라는 소유격이다. 이 둘은 완전히 다른 의미이기 때문에 정확히 구분해서 사용해야 한다.

→ **It's** my folder. (O)

Its my folder. (X)

4. lose와 loose의 차이

일반적으로 lose는 '잃어버리다'라는 뜻의 동사로서 <루즈>라고 발음하고, loose는 '느슨한' 혹은 '헐거운'이라는 뜻의 형용사로서 <루스>라고 발음한다.

→ Do not **lose** the key. (O)

Do not **loose** the key. (X)

→ These shirts are too **loose**. (O)

These shirts are too **lose**. (X)

41) 일반적으로 사용하는 부서명이지만 때로는 회사에 따라 다른 용어를 공식적으로 채택하는 경우도 있다.

5. conference와 meeting의 차이

meeting은 주로 사내 회의실에서 진행하는 소규모 회의를 말할 때 쓰이고, conference는 비교적 규모가 큰 회의 다시 말해 공식적인 행사를 지칭할 때 쓰인다.

→ Why don't we have a **meeting** at my office tomorrow? (O)
  Why don't we have a conference at my office tomorrow? (X)

6. eat dinner와 have dinner의 차이

구어체에서 '저녁을 먹다'라는 의미로 'eat dinner'라고 표현할 수 있지만, 비즈니스 문서에서는 이를 'have dinner'로 적는 것이 더 적합하다.

→ We are scheduled to **have dinner** at 6 PM. (O)
  We are scheduled to eat dinner at 6 PM. (△)

7. 'Excuse me'와 'Sorry'의 차이

'Excuse me'와 'Sorry'는 둘 다 '죄송합니다'라는 뜻이다. 그러나 'Excuse me'의 경우에는 사전에 '자신의 행동에 대해 양해를 구한다'는 의미를 가지고 있고, 'Sorry'는 사후적으로 자신이 한 행동에 대해 미안한 감정을 전달하는, 서로 다른 의미를 갖는다. 예를 들어 누군가에게 길을 묻거나 극장에서 사람들의 좌석을 지나 자신의 자리로 가는 상황에서는 'Excuse me'를 사용한다.

→ **Excuse me**, may I sit here?
  Sorry, I have not replied to you.

8. 'work' 앞에 붙는 수량형용사

'work'는 셀 수 없는 불가산명사기 때문에 앞에 many가 아니라 much가 온다.

→ I have **much work** to do. (O)
  I have many works to do. (X)

9. 'A.M 3:30'와 '3:30 A.M'의 차이

우리나라에서는 '오전 7시 30분'으로 표기하지만, 영어권 국가에서는 오전(A.M.)과 오후(P.M.)를 시간 뒤에 표기한다.

→ The meeting will be held at **3:30 P.M.** (O)
  The meeting will be held at P.M. 3:30. (X)

10. 괄호 안에 띄어쓰기

우리나라에서는 괄호를 바로 앞 단어와 붙여서 쓰는 습관이 있으나 영어권 국가에서는 이를 띄어 쓴다.

→ The managers from **Human Resources (HR)** are having a meeting. (O)

The managers from Human Resources(HR) are having a meeting. (X)

11. 'further'와 'farther'의 차이

further'는 정도를 나타낼 때 쓰이고, farther는 거리를 나타낼 때 쓰인다.

→ Everyday, she sinks **further** and **further** into depression. (점점 더 우울증에 빠져드는 상황)

→ My house is **farther** from work than yours. (직장에서 더 멀리 떨어져 있는 상황)

12. 'my'와 'our'의 차이

소유격의 사용과 관련하여, 한국인들은 '우리 사장님(our boss)' 혹은 '우리 직원(our employee)'과 같이 'my'보다 'our'를 주로 사용하지만, 이와 반대로 영어권 국가의 사람들은 일반적으로 'our' 대신에 'my'를 사용한다.

→ **My** boss will also be there. (O)

Our boss will also be there. (△)

13. 날짜 앞에서의 'on'과 'in'의 차이

on은 날짜나 요일, 특정한 날 앞에 쓰이고, in은 달이나 연도 앞에 쓰인다.

→ She will arrive **on** March 15.

We are waiting for the concert **on** Christmas Eve.

They will inspect the factory **in** December.

14. 한국식 콩글리시

단어	틀린 표현	올바른 표현
애프터 서비스	after service	**warranty service**
퀵 서비스	quick service	**courier = courier service**
스펙	spec	**qualification**
명함	name card	**business card**
핸드폰	handphone	**cellphone**
유에스비	USB	**USB stick (= memory stick)**

피티	PT	**presentation**
노트(공책)	note	**notebook**
할인	DC	**discount**
오티	OT	**orientation**
셀프	self	**self-service**
사인	sign	**signature**

Examples:

warranty service

→ The stove comes with a 1 year manufacturer's warranty service.

courier service

→ Some companies rely on a courier to deliver their packages.

= Some companies rely on a courier service to deliver their packages.

qualification

→ He is working towards his qualification to become a dentist.

business card

→ His business card was attached to his resume.

cellphone

→ I left my cell phone in my car.

USB stick = memory stick

→ I have the file on my USB stick

= I have the file on my memory stick.

presentation

→ The presentation was very short.

notebook

→ The plans were in the notebook.

discount

→ Only purchase the supplies if they are on discount.

orientation

→ Student orientation week is in September.

self-service

→ The gas station is self-service.

signature

→ A signature is required when receiving your package.

15. 거만한 느낌을 주는 표현은 피한다.

특정 영어표현이 갖는 뉘앙스를 잘 몰라서 본의 아니게 실수를 하는 경우가 있다. 예를 들면 <had better>의 경우가 그러하다. <had better>는 '~하는 게 좋겠다(낫겠다)'라는 사전적인 의미를 지니고 있지만, 실생활에서는 'must'의 의미 구체적으로 경고(warning)나 위협(threat)의 어조로 활용되기 때문이다. 따라서 나이가 많거나 지위가 높은 사람을 대상으로 하는 상황에서는 <had better> 대신에 <it would be better if ~>와 같은 완곡된 표현을 쓰는 것이 바람직하다.

> **<had better>** is more colloquial or conversational, in terms of wording.
>
> **<would be better if>** is more correct, than "had better" in terms of formality and proper grammar usage.

A supervisor to an employee:

→ You **had better** fix this fax machine by next week. (△)

= It **would be better for you** to fix this fax machine by next week. (△)

(다음 주까지 팩스기를 고치지 않으면 나중에 안 좋은 결과를 초래할 수 있다는 경고의 의미를 내포하기 때문에 강압적인 인상을 준다: 당장 '고쳐라'는 뉘앙스)

⬇

<수정>

It **would be better if** you fixed this fax machine by next week. (O)

= It **would be better if** you could fix this fax machine by next week. (O)

A parent talking to a child:

→ You **had better** finish up your homework before dinner! (O)

(숙제를 끝내지 않으면 나중에 안 좋은 결과를 초래할 수 있다는 경고의 의미를 내포하고 있지만 부모가 아이를 대상으로 하는 훈계로서는 적합한 표현이다: 당장 '숙제해라'는 뉘앙스)

Part 2 비즈니스 레터 작성시 자기 소개법

업무상 이메일을 처음 주고받을 때 자신에 대해 소개를 하는 것이 좋다. 이때 이름뿐만 아니라 자신의 정체성을 각인시켜 줄 담당부서와 회사명 등 세부 내용도 함께 소개한다.

1. 이름과 소속 부서 및 회사명을 소개할 때: <저는 ~회사 ~부서의 ~입니다>

→ 부서명 앞에 'from'을 쓰고 회사명 앞에 'at'를 쓴다.

I am	**이름**	**from**	**소속부서명**	**at**	**회사명**
This is	**이름**	**from**	**소속부서명**	**at**	**회사명**

Exercises:

▶ 저는 LG 마케팅부서의 Eric Song입니다.

→ ______________________________

▶ 저는 삼일 인사부의 Mike Kim입니다.

→ ______________________________

Answers:

▶ 저는 LG 마케팅부서의 Eric Song입니다.

→ **I am** Eric Song **from** the marketing department **at** LG.
This is Eric Song **from** the marketing department **at** LG.

▶ 저는 삼일 인사부의 Mike Kim입니다.

→ **I am** Mike Kim **from** the human resources department **at** Samil.
This is Mike Kim **from** the human resources department **at** Samil.

2. 맡은 업무를 중점적으로 소개할 때: <저는 ~업무를 담당하는 ~입니다>

① 저는 ~업무를 담당하는 ~입니다

I am 이름, **responsible for** 업무내용 **This is** 이름, **responsible for** 업무내용

Exercises:

저는 계약서 작성하는 일을 담당하는 Grace Hwang입니다.

→ ____

<write up>

저는 그 사안의 데이터를 기록하는 일을 담당하는 Andrew Simpson입니다.

→ ____

<recording / subject>

Answers:

저는 계약서 작성하는 일을 담당하는 Grace Hwang입니다.
<write up>

→ **I am** Grace Hwang, **responsible for** writing up contracts.
This is Grace Hwang, **responsible for** writing up contracts.

* 이 문장은 'responsible' 앞에 있던 'who is'가 생략된 것으로써 <주격관계대명사 + be동사>는 생략 가능하다.

* <responsible for> 대신에 <in charge of>를 써도 가능하다.

→ **I am** Grace Hwang, **in charge of** writing up contracts.
This is Grace Hwang, **in charge of** writing up contracts.

저는 그 사안의 데이터를 기록하는 일을 담당하는 Andrew Simpson입니다.
<recording / subject>

→ **I am** Andrew Simpson, **responsible for** recording the subject's data.
= **This is** Andrew Simpson, **in charge of** recording the subject's data.

② 저는 ~업무에 참여하고 있는 ~입니다.

I am	**이름, taking part in**	**업무내용**
This is	**이름, taking part in**	**업무내용**

Exercises:

저는 캐나다 프로젝트에 참여하고 있는 김현진입니다.

→ ______________________________

저는 연설자 포럼에 참여하고 있는 Benjamin Franklin입니다.

→ ______________________________

<speaker's forum>

Answers:

저는 캐나다 프로젝트에 참여하고 있는 김현진입니다.

→ **I am** Hyeonjin Kim, **taking part in** the Canada Project.
This is Hyeonjin Kim, **taking part in** the Canada Project.

* 이 문장은 'taking' 앞에 있던 'who is'가 생략된 것으로써 <주격관계대명사 + be동사>는 생략 가능하다.
* <taking part in> 대신에 <participating in>을 써도 가능하다.

→ **I am** Hyeonjin Kim, **participating in** the Canada Project[42)]
This is Hyeonjin Kim, **participating in** the Canada Project.

저는 연설자 포럼에 참여하고 있는 Benjamin Franklin입니다.
<speaker's forum>

→ **I am** Benjamin Franklin, **taking part in** the speaker's forum.
= **This is** Benjamin Franklin, **participating in** the speaker's forum.

---

42) If the name of the project is "Canada Project", then the "P" in Project needs to be capitalized. And if the name of the project includes "The", then the "T" needs to be capitalized:
<This is Grace Hwang, taking part in **the** Canada Project.>
<This is Grace Hwang, taking part in **The** Canada Project.>

3. 업무와 더불어 부서 및 회사를 소개할 때: <저는 ~회사 ~부서에서 ~을 담당하고 있는 ~입니다>

I am 이름, responsible for 업무내용 in/at 부서 at 회사 **This is 이름, responsible for 업무내용 in/at 부서 at 회사**

Exercises:

저는 두산 기획부에서 쿠바 프로젝트를 담당하고 있는 나도일입니다.

→ ______________________________

저는 ABC 사 광고부에서 LMB 상품을 담당하고 있는 Tom Jordon입니다.

→ ______________________________

Answers:

저는 두산 기획부에서 쿠바 프로젝트를 담당하고 있는 나도일입니다.

→ **I am** Doil Na, **responsible for** the Kuba Project **in/at** the planning department **at** Doosan.
= **This is** Doil Na, **responsible for** the Kuba Project **in/at** the planning department **at** Doosan.
* <Doosan> 앞에 전치사 <in>을 쓰면 틀린 문장이 된다.

저는 ABC 사 광고부에서 LMB 상품을 담당하고 있는 Tom Jordon입니다.

→ **I am** Tom Jordon, **responsible for** the LMB products **in/at** the advertising department **at** ABC Company.
= **This is** Tom Jordon, **responsible for** the LMB products **in/at** the advertising department **at** ABC Company.
* <ABC Company> 앞에 전치사 <in>을 쓰면 틀린 문장이 된다.

4. 나를 기억할 만한 단서를 제공하는 법

예전에 통화한 적이 있거나 한 번 만난 적이 있을 때 혹은 제3자를 통해서 연락처를 얻게 되었을 때, 나를 기억할 만한 단서를 제시하면 상대방에게 친밀감을 줄 수 있다.

① ~했던 경험에 대해 언급한다.

I am the one[44] who .... (저는 ~했던 사람입니다)

* 시중에 유통되고 있는 일부 교재들은 이와 동일한 문맥에서 <저는 ~했던 직원입니다>, 즉 **<I am the representative who ... >**라고 소개를 하고 있으나 자기 자신을 직원으로 소개하는 것은 어색한 표현이기 때문에 **<I am the one ...>** 이라고 적는 것이 올바르다.

Exercises:

🏴 저는 어제 전화로 주문에 대해 당신과 얘기를 나누었던 사람입니다.

→ ____

🏴 저는 일주일 전에 복사기 가격협상과 관련하여 전화드렸던 사람입니다.

→ ____

<regarding / negotiations for>

Answers:

🏴 저는 어제 전화로 주문에 대해 당신과 얘기를 나누었던 사람입니다.

→ I am the one **who spoke with you** about the order on the phone yesterday. (O)
= I am the one **you spoke with** on the phone about the order yesterday. (OO)
= I am the one **whom you spoke with** on the phone about the order yesterday.

* 위 문장에서 관계사절의 동사로 <talked>가 아닌 <spoke>를 사용한 것은 <talked>가 '누군가와 주고 받으며 대화하다'라는 의미의 비격식체 표현이라면, 이와 달리 <spoke>의 경우에는 말하는 행위에 초점을 둔, 다시 말해 누군가에게 말을 전달한다는 의미의 격식체 표현이기 때문이다. 따라서 다음 문장은 공식문서에 적합한 표현으로 볼 수 없다:

≠ I am the one you **talked with** on the phone about the order yesterday. **(Δ)**

* 위 문맥에서 전치사 <about>뿐만 아니라 전치사구 <in regards to>를 사용해도 올바른 문장이다.

→ I am the one you **spoke with** on the phone **in regards to** the order yesterday. **(O)**

---

43) 자신의 과거 경험에 대해 언급할 때에는 <I am the one ..>으로 표현하지만 제 3자를 상대방에게 소개할 때는 <This is the one ...>으로 표현한다.

Example: Here is Mary Grace …. This is the one (person) you spoke with about the order on the phone yesterday.

* <in regards to> 대신에 전치사 <on>을 사용할 경우에는 <the order> 앞에 <the subject of>를 적어야 올바른 문장이 된다. 따라서 위 문장에서 활용할 수 있는 가장 바람직한 전치사는 <about>와 <in regards to>라고 할 수 있다.

🏴 저는 일주일 전에 복사기 가격협상과 관련하여 전화드렸던 사람입니다.

<regarding / negotiations for>

→ I am the one who called you **regarding** the price negotiations for the copy machine one week ago.

= I am the one who called you **in regards to** the price negotiations for the copy machine one week ago.

* 위 문장에서 <in regards to> 대신에 전치사 <about>를 사용할 경우에는 <about> 앞에 <to speak>를 적어야 올바른 문장이 된다:

→ I am the one who called you **to speak about** the price negotiations for the copy machine one week ago.

② 만났던 경험에 대해 언급한다:

예전에 만난 경험이 있지만 서로 처음 연락하는 경우에는 자신(발신자)에 대한 기억을 떠올리게 할 만한 장소나 모임명에 대해 언급하는 것이 좋다.

This is 이름. We met at 장소/모임 이름 + 시간 (저는 ~입니다. 저희는 언제 ~에서 만났었습니다.)

Exercises:

🏴 저는 John Smith입니다. 지난 주 이사회에서 만났었지요.

→ ______________________________

<board meeting>

🏴 저는 Namid Miller입니다. 지난 9월 매니저 연수 세미나에서 만났었지요.

→ ______________________________

<Manager's Tranining Seminar>

Answers:

🏴 저는 John Smith입니다. 지난 주 이사회에서 만났었지요.

<board meeting>

→ This is John Smith. We met at the board meeting last week.

🏴 저는 Namid Miller입니다. 지난 9월 매니저 연수 세미나에서 만났었지요.
<Manager's Tranining Seminar>

→ This is Namid Miller. We met at the Manager's Tranining Seminar last September.

③ 소개해 준 사람에 대해 언급한다:

잘 모르는 사람의 이메일은 지나쳐 가거나 지워버릴 수가 있다. 그런데 상대방(수신자)이 잘 아는 사람으로부터 소개를 받아 연락을 하는 경우에는 소개한 사람의 이름을 언급함으로써 상대방으로 하여금 자신(발신자)에 대해 친밀감을 느끼도록 하는 것이 좋다.

a) ABC 세 사람이 서로 만난 적이 없는 상황에서 나에 대한 정보만 소개자에 의해서 간접적으로 상대방(수신자)에게 전달된 경우에는 '**be referred**'를 사용한다.

> I **was referred** (to you) **by** 소개자의 이름 **of/at** 소개자의 소속회사
> (~의 ~로부터 귀하를 소개받았습니다.)

Exercises:

🏴 KB 국민은행의 김종민 씨로부터 귀하를 소개받았습니다.
(세 사람이 서로 만난 적이 없는 상황)

→ ______________________________

🏴 삼성전자의 Brandon Wright 씨로부터 귀하를 소개받았습니다.
(세 사람이 서로 만난 적이 없는 상황)

→ ______________________________

Answers:

🏴 KB 국민은행의 김종민 씨로부터 귀하를 소개받았습니다.
(세 사람이 서로 만난 적이 없는 상황)

→ I **was referred** (to you) **by** Mr. Jongmin Kim **of** KB Kookmin Bank.
= I **was referred** (to you) **by** Mr. Jongmin Kim **at** KB Kookmin Bank.

🏴 삼성전자의 Brandon Wright 씨로부터 귀하를 소개받았습니다.
(세 사람이 서로 만난 적이 없는 상황)

→ I **was referred** (to you) **by** Mr. Brandon Wright **of** Samsung Electronics.
= I **was referred** (to you) **by** Mr. Brandon Wright **at** Samsung Electronics.

b) ABC 세 사람이 과거 어떤 장소에서 함께 만나서 (소개자에 의해서) **직접 소개를 주고받은 경우**에는 '**be introduced**'를 사용한다.

I **was introduced** (to you) **by** 소개자의 이름 **of/at** 소개자의 소속회사 (~의 ~로부터 귀하를 소개받았습니다.)

Exercises:

저는 귀사의 Winnie Burke 씨로부터 귀하를 소개받았습니다.
(과거에 세 사람이 같은 장소에서 만나서 소개자에 의해 직접 소개행위가 이루어진 상황)

→ ______________________________

저는 지난 주 만찬 모임에서 Lucas Jung 씨로부터 귀하를 소개받았습니다.
(과거에 세 사람이 같은 장소에서 만나서 소개자에 의해 직접 소개행위가 이루어진 상황)

→ ______________________________

<last week's dinner party>

Answers:

저는 귀사의 Winnie Burke 씨로부터 귀하를 소개받았습니다.
(과거에 세 사람이 같은 장소에서 만나서 소개자에 의해 소개행위가 이루어진 상황)

→ I **was introduced** to you **by** Ms. Winnie Burke **of** your company.
= I **was introduced** to you **by** Ms. Winnie Burke **at** your company.

저는 지난 주 만찬 모임에서 Lucas Jung 씨로부터 귀하를 소개받았습니다.
(과거에 세 사람이 같은 장소에서 만나서 소개자에 의해 직접 소개행위가 이루어진 상황)
<last week's dinner party>

→ I **was introduced** to you **by** Mr. Lucas Jung **of** last week's dinner party. (O)
= I **was introduced** to you **by** Mr. Lucas Jung **at** last week's dinner party. (O)
≠ I was introduced to you by Mr. Lucas Jung at **the** last week's dinner party. (**X**)
* 위 문맥에서 <at> 뒤에 관사 <the>를 붙이면 틀린 문장이 된다. 그러나 다음과 같이 수정하면 올바른 문장이 된다.

→ I was introduced to you by Mr. Lucas Jung **at the dinner party last week.** (O)

Fundamental Exercises

1. 다음 문장을 읽고 틀린 부분을 수정하여 전체 문장을 다시 쓰시오.

This is a self restaurant, so you will need to get your water from the counter.

→ ____

2. 다음 문장을 읽고 밑줄 친 부분에 적합한 단어를 적으시오.

The first priority is that you have to put the __________ into this computer. (우선적으로 해야 할 일은 당신이 USB를 이 컴퓨터에 넣어야 한다는 것이다.)

→ ______________________

3. <총무부>에 해당하는 부서명을 고르시오.

① department of logistics
② department of public relations
③ department of administration
④ department of human resources

4. 다음 문장을 영작하시오.

저는 IBT 사 마케팅부서에서 DMB 상품을 담당하고 있는 황남엽입니다.

→ ____

5. 다음 문장을 읽고 이에 적합한 영어문장을 고르시오.

삼진그룹의 황남엽 씨로부터 귀하를 소개받았습니다. (서로 만난 적이 없는 상황)

① I was referred to you by Ms. Namyeob Hwang within the Samjin Group.
② I was introduced to you through Ms. Namyeob Hwang at the Samjin Group.
③ I was introduced to you from Ms. Namyeob Hwang in the Samjin Group.
④ I was referred to you by Ms. Namyeob Hwang of the Samjin Group.

8장

영문 비즈니스 이메일 I - 항의 이메일

Email(전자우편)[44]은 일반 편지처럼 문자(text) 형태로 메시지를 주고 받는 것은 물론 사진과 음성의 송수신도 가능한 이점을 가지고 있다. 또한 시간과 장소의 장벽을 초월하여 동시에 여러 사람에게 메시지를 보낼 수 있고, 수신 이메일에 첨삭이 가능한 편리한 기능과 더불어 상대방과 신속하게 커뮤니케이션을 할 수도 있다. 이러한 이유에서 대부분의 직장인들은 업무처리와 관련하여 가장 빠르면서도 편리한 이메일을 사용하여 의사소통을 한다. 이렇듯 이메일은 직장 내에서 가장 빈번하게 쓰여지는 소통방식인 동시에 업무에 적극적으로 활용되고 있는 만큼 명확하고도 정확하게 작성될 필요가 있다. 일반적으로 비즈니스 이메일은 비즈니스 레터와 마찬가지로 경제활동과 관련되는 공식적인 문서의 일환이다. 따라서 영문 비즈니스 이메일을 작성할 때는 형식과 내용에 있어서 주의를 기울여야 한다. 이메일을 작성하는 방식은 비즈니스 영문 서신과 비슷하기 때문에 앞서 언급한 비즈니스 레터의 다섯 가지 기본원칙, 다시 말해 Clearness(명확성), Conciseness(간결성), Completeness(완전성), Courtesy(정중성), Correctness(정확성)을 토대로 작성해야 하며, 본론 구성 양식에 있어서도 비즈니스 레터의 본문양식에서 크게 벗어나지 않는다. 영문 비즈니스 이메일은 다음과 같이 포맷 구성요소와 본문 구성요소로 나누어 살펴볼 수 있다.

---

44) 이메일 ('electronic'과 'mail'의 복합명사)을 표기할 때 email과 e-mail 둘 다 사용할 수 있지만 짧고 간단한 용어인 email을 사용할 것을 추천한다.

Part 1 Format of a Business Email

1. From (발신자)

2. To (수신자)

자신이 받은 메일에 대해 회신을 해야 할 의무가 있다.

3. Date (발신 날짜)

날짜는 자동으로 생성된다.

4. Cc: (CC:) (참조)

Carbon Copy의 약자로, A에게 보내고자 하는 메일을 동시에 B,C,D 등에게 똑같이 보낼 때 사용한다. 수신자 입력방법과 관련하여, 1차 수신자(primary recipient)를 'To(받는 사람)'란(section)에 입력하고 2차 수신자(secondary recipients)는 'Cc:'란에 입력한다. 다시 말해 수신자로 A를 지정하고 참조인으로 B,C,D 등을 지정하면 A에게 보낸 이메일을 B,C,D 등이 함께 받게 되는 것이다. 이때 유의해야 할 점은 'Cc:' 기능과 더불어 보내는 이메일에서는 수신자가 누구인지 서로 알게 되어 결국 서로에게 이메일 주소까지 모두 공개가 되기 때문에 개인정보 노출과 관련하여 신경을 써야 할 필요가 있다. 참고로 참조인은 자신이 받은 메일에 대해 회신할 의무는 없으며 참조인이 다수일 경우, 그들의 주소를 부서나 직급의 높은 순서대로 정렬하여 입력하는 것이 좋고, 세미콜론(;)이나 쉼표(,)를 사용하여 그들의 주소를 분리하여 보낸다.

5. Bcc: (BCC:) (숨은 참조)

→ 여러 사람에게 동시에 이메일을 보내야 하는 상황에서 이메일을 받는 사람이 누구인지 알리고 싶지 않을 때 사용한다.

Blind Carbon Copy의 약자로, A에게 보내고자 하는 이메일을 동시에 B,C,D 등에게 똑같이 보낼 때 사용한다. 수신자 입력방법과 관련하여, 1차 수신자를 'To'란에 입력하고 개인정보(이름 및 이메일 주소)를 알리고 싶지 않은 나머지 수신자들을 'Bcc:'란에 입력한다. 다시 말해 A를 수신자로 그리고 B,C,D 등을 숨은 참조인으로 지정하면 A에게 보낸 이메일을 B,C,D 등이 함께 받게 되는 것이다. 'Bcc:' 기능을 사용하여 이메일을 보내면 1차 수신자는 숨은 참조인들의 이름과 이메일 주소를 볼 수 없고, 숨은 참조인들의 경우에도 자신이 받은 메일을 (1차 수신자를 제외하고) 누가 또 받았는지 알 수 없기 때문에 서로 간의 개인정보를 노출시키지 않는다는 이점을 갖는다.

6. Fwd: (FWD: = Fw: = FW:) (전달)

'Forward'의 줄임말로서 본인이 받은 메일을 다른 사람에게 그대로 전달할 때 사용한다.

7. Subject (제목)

이메일 제목 작성 방식과 관련하여, 제목만 읽어도 개괄적인 본문 내용을 짐작할 수 있도록 구체적이고도 명확하게 기입하는 것이 좋다. 또한 서신의 용건을 한 눈에 알 수 있도록 (가급적 여덟 단어 이하로) 간단명료하게 작성하고 가능한 제목의 길이는 35개 글자수를 넘지 않을 것을 권한다. 대문자 규칙과 관련해서는, 전통적으로 제목을 대문자로 표기하는 것을 원칙으로 하고 있으나, 제목의 길이가 긴 경우에는 소문자로 기재해도 무방하다.

examples:
Thank You for the Interview (면접에 대한 감사 연락)
Recommendation Letter Request (추천서 요청에 대한 연락)
The Next Meeting[46] (다음 회의에 대한 연락)
[Urgent] The bug[47] fix doesn't work properly. 버그 수정이 제대로 안됩니다. (긴급사항에 대한 연락)

8. Re: (RE:) (답장)

'Re:'는 'reply'의 약어로서 일반적으로 'Reply' 다시 말해 '답장' 혹은 '답신'의 의미로 활용된다. 이메일을 보낼 때 답장 버튼을 클릭하면 제목란에 자동적으로 'Re:'가 뜬다.

9. Attachments (첨부파일)

각종 문서파일이나 그림파일 혹은 음성파일을 첨부할 때 사용한다.

10. P.S. (추신)

'P.S.'는 'Postscript'의 약어로서 이메일을 다 쓰고 나서 추가로 하나의 문장이나 단락을 넣을 때 사용된다. P.S는 주로 개인과 개인 간에 주고 받는 이메일에서 쓰여지기 때문에 격식을 갖추어야 하는 비즈니스 이메일에서는 사용하지 않을 것을 추천한다. 참고로, 추신을 하나 더 추가하는 경우에는 'PPS(post post scriptum)'로 표기한다.

45) 'the'를 생략하고 기재할 수 있다 : personal choice of the writer.

46) 기계결함, 컴퓨터 바이러스

Part 2 How to Write a Business Email

영문 비즈니스 이메일의 본론 구성요소와 작성법은 영문 비즈니스 레터의 것들과 비슷하다. 이메일을 작성할 때에는 겸손하고 부드러운 어조로 자신이 쓰고자 하는 내용을 가급적 짧은 문장과 평이한 언어를 사용하여 간결하면서도 명확하게 전달한다. 긍정적인 어조로 가급적 자신의 감정을 배제한 객관적인 입장에서 서술해야 하며 문어체와 구어체를 혼합하여 사용하는 것도 좋다. 자신의 품격을 갖추면서도 자신의 진심이 상대방에게 전달될 수 있도록 예의를 갖추어 작성하는 것이 중요한데, 그 과정에서 유행어, 약어, 속어를 사용하지 말아야 한다. 또한 작성방식과 관련하여, 왼쪽 정렬을 기준으로 하는 것이 보편적이며, 단락과 단락 사이에는 한 줄을 띄우고, 수동태 문장보다는 능동태 문장을 사용할 것을 권고한다. 나아가 나열할 여러 항목들이 있을 경우에는 불릿포인트(bullet point)를 사용하는 것이 좋다.

1. 인사말 (Salutation)

받는 사람 이름을 기재할 때 보편적으로 이름 앞에 Dear를 쓰고, 이름 뒤에 콜론(:)을 붙이거나 콤마(,)를 붙이기도 한다. 콜론은 매우 격식 있는 표현으로서 상대방이 높은 직위에 있거나 중요한 이메일을 처음 보낼 때 사용한다.

① 수신자의 성별과 이름을 아는 경우, Dear 다음에 경칭(Mr. Mrs. Miss. Ms,)을 쓰고 성명을 기재한다.

Dear Mr. Gordon Soo: (OO)

Dear Mr. Soo: (O)

* 경칭(Mr) 다음에 수신자의 전체이름을 기재하는 것이 좋다.

② 수신자의 성별과 결혼유무에 대해 모르는 경우, Dear 다음에 상대방의 성명을 기재한다.

Dear Alex Park:

③ 수신자의 이름을 모르는 경우, Dear 다음에 직함 예를 들어 "Dear Hiring Manager:" 혹은 "Dear General Manager:"라고 적는다. 또한 Dear 다음에 "Sir/Madam:"을 쓰기도 하고, "To Whom It May Concern:"이라고 기재할 수도 있다.

Dear Hiring Manager:
Dear General Manager:
Dear Sir:
Dear Madam:
To Whom It May Concern:

④ 발신자와 수신자가 서로 아는 관계에서는 'Dear' 나 'Hello (Hi)' 다음에 이름을 쓰고 쉼표를 붙여도 된다: <Dear Ruth,> <Hi Ruth,>

2. 서론 (Introduction Paragraph)

상대방에게 처음 이메일을 보내는 경우에는 첫 단락에서 간단하게 자기소개를 해야겠지만 이미 이전에 연락을 주고 받았던 사이에서는 일반적으로 자기소개 없이 단도직입적으로 바로 본문 내용으로 들어가도 된다.

3. 본론 (Body Paragraph)

이메일에서 가장 중요한 것은 신속함과 간결함이다. 따라서 최대한 간단하고 명료한 문장과 더불어 분량이 길어지지 않도록 압축해서 작성하는 것이 좋다. 내용과 관련하여, 본론에서 발신자의 의도라고 할 수 있는 메일의 주제(목적)를 전달해야 하기 때문에 이를 뒷받침할 수 있는 세부사항을 포함하여 보다 구체적으로 전달한다. 또한 앞서 언급한 것처럼, 이메일을 작성할 때에는 문어체와 일상적인 구어체를 혼합하여 사용할 수 있다. 그러나 문체와 관련하여 한 가지 알아두어야 할 것은, 구어체 사용이 가능하다고는 하지만 최소한의 격식과 예의는 갖추어서 글을 써야 한다는 것이다. 이것은 공식적으로 얼마만큼 격식을 갖추어야 할지 또 얼마만큼 격식을 갖추지 않아도 되는지에 대한 고민의 필요성을 방증하는 대목이기도 하다. 영어에는 높임말이 없다고 하지만 친구 사이에서나 쓸 만한 너무 격의 없는, 지나치게 구어체적인 표현은 피해야 하기 때문이다.

▶ 격식을 갖추지 않은 예:

Hey Grace,
Just wanted to chat about that new invoice that you mentioned two weeks ago. Let's meet up and figure out the details. Does next week work for you? Your office would work better than mine.

▶ 지나치게 격식을 갖춘 예:

Ms. Grace,
When you have some extra time, I' d like to request that we meet again to hear your explanation of the new invoice that was discussed two weeks ago. Please let me know of a convenient time for you. If it would be suitable, I would like to visit your office sometime next week.

▶▶ 원어민 관점에서 본 바람직한 표현:

Hey Grace,
Would it be possible to meet with you regarding the new invoice that we discussed two weeks ago? It would be great to meet in-person to discuss it's details. If next week works for you, we can meet at your office.

4. 결론 (Concluding Paragraph)

상대방에게 요청을 하거나 부탁하고 싶은 내용에 대해 언급하면서 너무 길지 않은 2~3줄의 내용으로 마무리한다.

5. 끝인사 (Closing)

본론을 끝낸 후에 인사처럼 쓰는 말이다. 특별한 뜻은 없고 '감사합니다' 정도로 보면 된다.

일반적인 비즈니스 서신	Sincerely, Sincerely yours, Yours sincerely,
격식을 차려야 하는 공식적인 비즈니스 서신	Truly yours, Yours truly,
정부관료나 대학교수에게 보내는 비즈니스 서신	Respectfully, Respectfully yours, Yours respectfully,
친분이 있는 직장 동료나 부하직원에게 보내는 비즈니스 서신	Best regards, Regards, Best wishes,

6. 서명 (Signature): 자필서명 — 선택사항

7. 서명란 (Signature block)

서명란은 이메일의 맨 마지막에 발신자의 이름과 연락처, 기타 관련 정보를 첨부하는 것을 말한다. 이곳에 발신자의 소속부서, 전화번호, 팩스번호, 홈페이지 등을 필요로 따라 추가한다. 이때 서명란에 해당하는 내용을 이메일용 프로그램에 등록해두면 영문 이메일을 쓸 때 편리하다.

① 이름과 회사명만 간단히 쓰는 경우

Namyeob Hwang
C&G Co.

② 이름, 직책, 부서명, 회사명 및 연락처 표기[47] – 가장 일반적인 경우

Namyeob Hwang, Manager (이름 + 직책)
Marketing Department (부서)
C&G Co. (회사명)
phone number of company (연락처)

③ 모든 정보를 표기하는 경우

(+ 회사의 전화번호, 팩스번호, 이메일 주소, 회사 홈페이지까지 명시)

Namyeob Hwang, Manager
Marketing Department
C&G Co.
+82-2-914-1234 (direct)
+82-2-914-0123 (fax)
marygrace@hanmail.net
http://www.C&G.com

---

47) 수신자로부터 연락을 받아야 하는 경우에는 연락처를 기재하는 것이 좋다:
Jeniffer Hwang, Secretary
________ Middle School
phone number of school

Part 3 How to Write a Complaint Email

항의 이메일(complaint email)은 주로 사용한 제품/서비스와 관련하여 발생한 불만/문제[48]에 대해 항의를 제기하는 문서이다. 작성과정에서 유의할 것은 발신자의 불유쾌한 감정이 드러나지 않도록 보다 객관적이고도 사무적인 어조로 정중하면서도 단호하게 써야 한다는 점이다. 항의 이메일은 단순히 상대방에 대해 비난을 표현하는 것이 아니라 문제해결 방법을 제시하고 해명에 대한 요청과 더불어 보상을 이끌어 내는 목적이 더 크기 때문이다. 따라서 객관적인 사실 및 상황을 정확하게 파악하고 이를 근거로 한 불만사항을 구체적으로 서술해야 하며, 상대방이 수긍할 수 있도록 논리적이고도 차분하게 메시지를 작성할 필요가 있다. 경우에 따라서는 합리적인 대안을 제시하는 것도 바람직하다.

*** 항의 이메일 작성방법은 다음과 같다.**

① **제목** (Subject) : 항의하고자 하는 내용이 무엇인지 명확히 알 수 있도록 키워드를 넣어서 간단명료하게 제목을 작성한다.

② **서론** (Introduction Paragraph) : 이메일을 보내는 목적의 일환으로 발생한 문제가 무엇인지에 대해 간략하게 명시한다.

③ **본론** (Body Paragraph) : 발생한 문제가 무엇인지에 대해 구체적으로 기술한다. 언제, 어떻게 문제가 발생했는지에 대해 언급하면서 문제 제기의 원인이 된 제반 사실에 대해 객관적으로 제시한다. 나아가 이로 인해 입게 되는 손해가 무엇인지에 대해서도 최대한 자세하게 설명한다.

④ **결론** (Closing Paragraph) : 자신의 요구사항 다시 말해 자신이 원하는 상대방의 대처 방안에 대해 명확하게 기술한다.

48) 불만사항이 있는 경우에는 'complaint'을 사용하고, 불만사항의 전 단계에서 문제가 있다는 것을 알려야 하는 상황에서는 'problem'을 사용한다.

Part 4 Example of a Business Email: Complaint Email

항의 이메일

제목: 배송된 우유의 유통기한

Ann Smith 씨에게

오늘 하루도 잘 지내시기를 바랍니다. 저는 CBL 베이커리에 근무하는 제이 김입니다. 어제 아침 (2022년 5월 21일), 우리가 귀사에 주문했던 우유 100통을 받았습니다. 하지만 저희는 그 중 우유 30통의 유통기한이 이미 지났었다는 것을 알게 되었습니다.

어제 저희가 주문한 것을 받았을 때, 우유 70통은 양호한 상태로 도착했지만 나머지 30통은 5월 19일자 유통기한이었습니다. 저희 베이커리는 가장 신선한 유제품만을 사용하는 것에 자부심을 가지고 있기 때문에, 앞서 언급한 우유 30통을 사용할 수 없었습니다. 결과적으로, 저희는 저희의 가장 인기 있는 프레첼(의) 생산에 있어서의 지연에 직면하게 되었고, 결국 최소 2천 달러의 수익손실을 초래하였습니다.

저는 귀사가 이 불미스러운 사건에 대해 어떻게 보상해줄 수 있는지에 대해 당신으로부터 답변을 듣기를 바랍니다. 가능한 빨리 604-914-1234로 연락주세요.

감사합니다.

Jay Kim

Jay Kim, Manager
Administration Department
CLB Bakery
604-914-1234

<English Words and Idioms>

deliver 배송하다
expiration date of ~의 유통기한

100 cartons of milk 우유 100 통
order from ~에서 주문하다.
discover 알게 되다.
expire (기한이) 지나다.

order 주문한 물건
good condition 양호한 상태
remaining 남아있는
since ~ 때문에
take pride in ~에 자부심을 가지다.
dairy products 유제품
mention 언급하다.
as a result 결과적으로
face (위험에) 직면하다
delay in ~의 지연
eventually 결국
bring about ~을 초래하다, ~을 야기시키다(~을 유발하다) = result in
lost income 수익손실

hope to hear from ~로부터 답변을 듣기를 바란다. (연락주기를 바란다)
unfortunate 불미스러운
incident 사건
compensate for ~에 대해 보상하다.
contact 연락하다.
as soon as possible 가능한 빨리

Part 5 영작연습

다음 문장을 영작하시오.

제목: 배송된 우유의 유통기한

→ ______________________

<delivered / expiration date>

Ann Smith 씨에게

→ ____________

1. The First Paragraph

오늘 하루도 잘 지내시기를 바랍니다.

→ ______________________

<hope / well>

저는 CBL 베이커리에 근무하는 제이 김입니다.

→ ______________________

<this is / from>

어제 아침 (2022년 5월 21일), 우리가 귀사에 주문했던 우유 100통을 받았습니다.

→ ____

<100 cartons of milk / order from>

하지만 저희는 그 중 우유 30통의 유통기한이 이미 지났었다는 것을 알게 되었습니다.

→ ____

<however / discover / expiration date of / expire>

2. The Second Paragraph

어제 저희가 주문한 것을 받았을 때, 우유 70통은 양호한 상태로 도착했지만 나머지 30통은 5월 19일자 유통기한이었습니다.

→ ____

____

<received / the order / good condition / remaining / had / expiration date of>

저희 베이커리는 가장 신선한 유제품만을 사용하는 것에 자부심을 가지고 있기 때문에, 앞서 언급한 우유 30통을 사용할 수 없었습니다.

→ ____

____

<since / take pride in / dairy products / mentioned>

결과적으로, 저희는 저희의 가장 인기 있는 프레첼(의) 생산에 있어서의 지연에 직면하게 되었고, 결국 최소 2천 달러의 수익손실을 초래하였습니다.

→ ____

____

<as a result / face / a delay in / eventually / bring about / in lost income>

3. The Third Paragraph

저는 귀사가 이 불미스러운 사건에 대해 어떻게 보상해줄 수 있는지에 대해 당신으로부터 답변을 듣기를 바랍니다.

→ ____

____

<hope to hear from / compensate for / unfortunate / incident>

가능한 빨리 604-914-1234로 연락주세요.

→ ____________________________________

<as soon as possible / contact>

감사합니다.

→ __________

Jay Kim, Manager
Administration Department
CLB Bakery
604-914-1234

Part 6 정답과 해설

제목: 배송된 우유의 유통기한

<delivered / expiration date>

→ Subject: Expiration date **of** the milk delivered

= Expiration date **for** the milk delivered **(△)**

* 'Expiration date' 뒤에 <for>를 쓰면 완전히 틀린 표현이라고는 할 수 없지만 <of>를 쓰는 것이 더 정확한 표현이다.

Ann Smith 씨에게

→ Dear Ms, Ann Smith:

1. The First Paragraph

오늘 하루도 잘 지내시기를 바랍니다.

<hope / well>

→ I hope you are well today.

저는 CBL 베이커리에 근무하는 제이 김입니다.

<this is / from>

→ This is Jay Kim from CBL Bakery.

= This is Jay Kim **with** CBL Bakery.

* 소개하는 장소에 본인이 직접 있는 경우에는 다음과 같이 전치사 <at>을 써도 가능하다:

= This is Jay Kim **at** CBL Bakery.

어제 아침 (2022년 5월 21일), 우리가 귀사에 주문했던 우유 100통을 받았습니다.

<100 cartons of milk / order from>

→ Yesterday Morning (May 21, 2022), we received the 100 cartons of milk **that** we ordered from your company. (O)

* 앞에 한정되어 있는 표현(100 cartons of milk)이 있기 때문에 <that>는 (뒤에서 명사를 수식하는 형용사 역할을 하는) 관계대명사의 한정적 용법이다

≠ Yesterday Morning (May 21, 2022), we received the 100 cartons of milk **which** we ordered from your company. **(X)**

* 원어민 시각으로 보면 which가 삽입된 위 문장은 틀린 표현이라고 한다. 이것과 관련하여, 근래에 들어서 북미에서 주로 사용되는 관계대명사는 <which>가 아니라 <that>이라는 것도 더불어 알아두기 바란다.

하지만 저희는 그 중 우유 30통의 유통기한이 이미 지났었다는 것을 알게 되었습니다.

<however / discover / expiration date of / expire>

→ However, we discovered that the expiration date **of** the 30 cartons of milk among them had already expired. (O)

* <Expiration date>' 뒤에 <for>를 쓰면 완전히 틀린 표현이라고 할 수 없지만 <of>를 쓰는 것이 더 정확한 표현이다.

However, we discovered that the expiration date **for** the 30 cartons of milk among them had already expired. (△)

2. The Second Paragraph

어제 저희가 주문한 것을 받았을 때, 우유 70통은 양호한 상태로 도착했지만 나머지 30통은 5월 19일자 유통기한이었습니다.

<received / the order / good condition / remaining / had / expiration date of>

→ When we received the order yesterday, 70 cartons of milk arrived in good condition but the remaining 30 cartons had an expiration date of May 19.

* <70 cartons of milk> 앞에 'the'를 붙이면 틀린 문장이 된다.
* <expiration date> 뒤에 'for'를 붙이면 어색한 문장이 된다.

= When we received the order **of 100 milk cartons** yesterday, **70 of the cartons** arrived in good condition **while 30 of the cartons** had an expiration date of May 19.

= When we received the order yesterday, 70 cartons of milk arrived in good condition, **aside from 30 of the cartons having already expired. These cartons have an expiration date of May 19**.

저희 베이커리는 가장 신선한 유제품만을 사용하는 것에 자부심을 가지고 있기 때문에, 앞서 언급한 우유 30통을 사용할 수 없었습니다.

<since / take pride in / dairy products / mentioned>

→ Since our bakery takes pride in using only the freshest dairy products, we could not use the mentioned 30 cartons of milk.

결과적으로, 저희는 저희의 가장 인기 있는 프레첼(의) 생산에 있어서의 지연에 직면하게 되었고, 결국 최소 2천 달러의 수익손실을 초래하였습니다.

<as a result / face / a delay in / eventually / bring about / in lost income>

→ As a result, we faced a delay in production of our most popular Pretzels, and eventually **brought about** at least 2,000 dollars in lost income.

= As a result, we faced a delay in production of our most popular Pretzels, **which** eventually **resulted in** at least 2,000 dollars in lost income.

* 이 문장에서 which의 선행사는 절(clause), 즉 앞 문장 전체이다.

= As a result, **we are now facing a delay in the production of our prized Pretzels, with an estimated $2000 in lost income.**

3. The Third Paragraph

저는 귀사가 이 불미스러운 사건에 대해 어떻게 보상해줄 수 있는지에 대해 당신으로부터 답변을 듣기를 바랍니다.

<hope to hear from / compensate for / unfortunate / incident>

→ I hope to hear from you about how your company can compensate for this unfortunate incident.

= I hope to hear **back** from you about how your company can compensate for this unfortunate incident.

* **완곡된 표현**: I'd like to speak with you regarding this unfortunate incident.

가능한 빨리 604-914-1234로 연락주세요.

<as soon as possible / contact>

→ As soon as possible, please contact me at 604-914-1234.

= Please contact me as soon as possible at 604-914-1234.

* 캐나다 밴쿠버 지점 베이커리 회사와 동일한 지역에 있는 우유회사와의 거래인 경우에도 밴쿠버 지역번호 (604)를 기재한 후 연락처를 적는다.

감사합니다.

→ Sincerely,

Jay Kim, Manager
Administration Department
CLB Bakery
604-914-1234

Part 7 Final Draft

Subject: Expiration date of the milk delivered

Dear Ms. Ann Smith:

I hope you are well today. This is Jay Kim from CLB Bakery. Yesterday morning (May 21, 2022), we received the 100 cartons of milk that we ordered from your company. However we discovered that the expiration date of the 30 cartons of milk among them had already expired.

When we received the order yesterday, 70 cartons of milk arrived in good condition but the remaining 30 cartons had an expiration date of May 19. Since our bakery takes pride in using only the freshest dairy products, we could not use the mentioned 30 cartons of milk. As a result, we faced a delay in production of our most popular Pretzels, and eventually brought about at least 2,000 dollars in lost income.

I hope to hear from you about how your company can compensate for this unfortunate incident. Please contact me as soon as possible at 604-914-1234.

Sincerely,

Jay Kim, Manager
Administration Department
CLB Bakery
604-914-1234

Part 8 Native English Speaker's Revision for the Final Draft

Subject: Expiration date of our milk **delivery**

Dear Ms. Ann Smith:

I hope you are well today. This is Jay Kim from CLB Bakery. Yesterday morning (May 21, 2022), we received the 100 cartons of milk that we ordered from your company. They arrived in good condition, **aside from 30 of the cartons having already expired. These cartons have an expiration date of May 19.**

Our bakery prides itself on food safety and food health, using only the freshest ingredients. We are unable to use these expired cartons in our production line. As a result, we are now facing a delay in the production of our prized pretzels, with an estimated $2000 in lost income.

I'd like to speak with you regarding this unfortunate incident. Please contact me as soon as possible at 604-914-1234.

Sincerely,

Jay Kim, Manager
Administration Department
CLB Bakery
604-914-1234

Fundamental Exercises

1. BCC란 무엇인가?

① 참조 ② 제목 ③ 전달 ④ 숨은 참조

2. 다음 문장을 올바르게 수정하여 전체 문장을 다시 쓰시오.

When we received the order yesterday, 70 cartons of milk arrived in good condition but the remained 30 cartons had an expiration date of May 19.
(어제 저희가 주문한 것을 받았을 때, 우유 70통은 양호한 상태로 도착했지만 나머지 30통은 5월 19일자 유통기한이었습니다.)

→ ____________________

____

3. 다음 문장을 읽고 밑줄 친 부분에 적합한 단어를 적으시오.

However, we discovered that the ____________ the 30 cartons of milk among them had already expired.
(하지만 저희는 그 중 우유 30통의 유통기한이 이미 지났었다는 것을 알게 되었습니다.)

→ ____________________

4. 다음 문장에서 밑줄 친 부사절(adverbial clause)을 해석하시오.

Since our bakery takes pride in using only the freshest dairy products, we could not use the mentioned 30 cartons of milk.

→ ____________________

5. 다음 밑줄 친 관계대명사(which)의 선행사를 고르시오.

As a result, we faced a delay in production of our most popular Pretzels, which eventually resulted in at least 2,000 dollars in lost income.

① our most popular Pretzels ② production
③ we faced a delay in production of our most popular Pretzels
④ delay

9장

영문 비즈니스 이메일 II - 감사 이메일

직장생활을 하면서 감사 이메일을 보내는 상황은 다양하다. 해외출장을 하면서 신세를 졌다거나 누군가로부터 필요로 하는 파일을 받았을 때와 같이 여러 다양한 경우들이 있다. 이렇듯 고마움을 전해야 하는 상황에서 신세를 진 내용에 대한 언급과 더불어, 감사 이메일을 보내면 상대방에게 예의 바른 사람이라는 좋은 인상을 심어줄 수 있다. 영문 이메일에서 정해진 서론 표현이 있는 것은 아니지만 이에 해당하는 일반적인 패턴으로는 <~해 주셔서 감사합니다>가 있다.

> **thank you for + 명사** 혹은 **동명사**
> **appreciate + 명사** 혹은 **동명사**
>
> ** **보충설명**:
>
> They are both correct, but have slightly different meanings. The first phrase is directly thanking them for something. The second phrase is to say that you value something. They are both positive sentiments though, so can both be used.

Exercises:

⚑ 귀하의 친절에 감사드립니다.

→ ____

⚑ 저를 취업면접에 초대해 주셔서 감사합니다.

→ ____

<job interview>

⚑ 저를 도와주셔서 감사합니다.

→ ____

⚑ 제 보고서를 도와주셔서 감사합니다.

→ ____

Answers:

⚑ 귀하의 친절에 감사드립니다.

→ **Thank you for** your **kindness.**
= I really **appreciate** your **kindness.**

** **보충설명:** They have slightly different meanings. The first sentence is directly thanking them for being kind. The second sentence is to say that you value their kindness. They are both positive sentiments, and can both be used.

⚑ 저를 취업면접에 초대해 주셔서 감사합니다.
<job interview>
→ I **thank you for** invit**ing** me to the job interview.
= I really **appreciate your** invit**ing** me to the job interview.
≠ I really appreciate inviting me to the job interview. (X)

** **보충설명:** They have slightly different meanings. The first sentence is more direct, It is always better to say "thank you". The second sentence is more passive

→ I am really **thankful/grateful for**[49] **your** invit**ing** me to the job interview.
→ I **am writing to thank you for** inviting me to the job interview.
≠ I am writing to appreciate your inviting me to the job interview. (X)

⚑ 저를 도와주셔서 감사합니다.

→ **Thank you for** helping me.
= **I really appreciate** your helping me.
≠ **I really appreciate** helping me. (X)

⚑ 제 보고서를 도와주셔서 감사합니다.

→ Thank you for **helping with** my report. (O)
= Thank you for **helping me with** my report. (O)
≠ Thank you for helping my report. (X)
* <help>의 목적어가 사람인 경우에는 전치사 없이 바로 목적어(사람)가 오지만, 사물인 경우에는 전치사 <with>를 붙이고 목적어(사물)를 쓴다:
examples: My boss asked his representatives to **help** him with his English presentation.
= My boss asked his workers to **help with** his English presentation.

= **I really appreciate** your help**ing with** my report. (O)

49) 전치사 of를 사용하면 틀린 문장이 된다.

Part 1 Example of a Business Email: Thank You Email

상대방으로부터 어떤 도움을 받았을 때 간단한 문장이라도 가급적 빨리 고마운 마음을 담아 감사 이메일을 보내는 것이 좋다. 간단하고 명료한 문장과 더불어 분량은 길어지지 않도록 간결하게 작성한다. 상대방에게 감사의 마음을 전하고 어떤 도움을 받았는지에 대해 구체적으로 언급하면서 친근하면서도 예의를 갖춘 내용으로 마무리한다.

감사 이메일

제목: 당신의 환대에 감사드립니다.

Brown 씨에게

이틀 전 당신의 공장을 방문했을 때, 제게 베풀어주신 당신의 환대에 감사를 드리고자 글을 씁니다. 당신의 명확하고도 자세한 설명 덕택에, 제가 ABC 프로젝트를 수월하게 끝마칠 수 있었습니다. 당신의 공장을 방문하는 동안, 저에 대한 당신의 배려에 다시 한 번 감사드립니다. 제게 필요한 것이 있으시면, 편하게 언제든지 연락주십시요. 곧 뵙기를 바랍니다.

안녕히 계세요

Greg Kim

<English Words and Idioms>

thank you for 명사 ~에 대해 감사드립니다.
hospitality 환대 (접대)
factory 공장
extend 베풀다
thanks to ~ 덕택에
clear 명확한
detailed 자세한
once again 다시 한 번, 거듭
consideration 배려
during ~하는 동안
visit 방문
If there is anything you need from me 제게 필요한 것이 있으시면
= Should there be anything you may need from me
feel free 편하게
at any time 언제든지

Part 2. 영작연습

다음 문장을 영작하시오.

감사 이메일

→ ______________________________

제목: 당신의 환대에 감사드립니다.

→ ______________________________

<hospitality>

Brown 씨에게

→ _______________

<Ms.>

이틀 전 당신의 공장을 방문했을 때, 제게 베풀어주신 당신의 환대에 감사를 드리고자 글을 씁니다.

→ ____

<thank you for / extend / factory>

당신의 명확하고도 자세한 설명 덕택에, 제가 ABC 프로젝트를 수월하게 끝마칠 수 있었습니다.

→ ____

<thanks to / detailed / be able to>

당신의 공장을 방문하는 동안, 저에 대한 당신의 배려에 다시 한 번 감사드립니다.

→ ____

<once again / thank you for / consideration / during / visit / at>

제게 필요한 것이 있으시면, 편하게 언제든지 연락주십시오.

→ ____

<if there is anything you need from me / feel free / contact>

곧 뵙기를 바랍니다.

→ ________________________

<hope>

안녕히 계세요

→ ____________

Greg Kim

Part 3 정답과 해설

감사 이메일

→ Thank You Email

제목: 당신의 환대에 감사드립니다.

<hospitality>

→ Subject: Thank You for Your Hospitality

Brown 씨에게

<Ms.>

→ Dear Ms. Brown,

이틀 전 당신의 공장을 방문했을 때, 제게 베풀어주신 당신의 환대에 감사를 드리고자 글을 씁니다.

<thank you for / extend / factory>

→ I am writing to thank you for your hospitality you extended me when I visited your factory two days ago.

= I **would like to express my deep gratitude for** your hospitality you extended to me when I visited your factory two days ago.

당신의 명확하고도 자세한 설명 덕택에, 제가 ABC 프로젝트를 수월하게 끝마칠 수 있었습니다.

<thanks to / detailed / be able to>

→ Thanks to your clear and detailed explanations, I was able to easily finish the ABC Project,

= **Because of** your clear and detailed explanations, I **could** easily finish the ABC Project,

당신의 공장을 방문하는 동안, 저에 대한 당신의 배려에 다시 한 번 감사드립니다.

<once again / thank you for / consideration / during / visit / at>

→ Once again, I thank you for your consideration of me during my visit at your factory.

= **During my visit at your factory**, once again, I thank you for your consideration of me.

제게 필요한 것이 있으시면, 편하게 언제든지 연락주십시오.

<if there is anything you need from me / feel free / contact>

→ If there is anything you need from me, please feel free to contact me at any time.

= **Should** there **be** anything you **may** need from me, please feel free to contact me at any time.

곧 뵙기를 바랍니다.
<hope>
→ I hope to see you soon.

안녕히 계세요
→ Sincerely,

Greg Kim

Part 4 Final Draft

Thank You Email

Subject: Thank You for Your Hospitality

Dear Ms. Brown,

I am writing to thank you for the hospitality you extended me when I visited your factory two days ago. Thanks to your clear and detailed explanations, I was able to easily finish the ABC Project. Once again, I thank you for your consideration of me during my visit at your factory. Should there be anything you may need from me, please feel free to contact me at any time. I hope to see you soon.

Sincerely,

Greg Kim

Part 5 Native English Speaker's Revision for the Thank You Email

Thank You Email

Subject: Thank You for Your Hospitality

Dear Ms. Brown,

I would like to express my deep gratitude for the hospitality you extended to me when I visited your factory two days ago. **Because of** your clear and detailed explanations, I was able to easily finish the ABC Project.

Should there be anything you may need from me, please feel free to contact me at any time. **It would be my honor to be of assistance.**[50)]

I hope to see you soon.

Sincerely,

Greg Kim

50) <It would be my honor to be of assistance>는 관용어구로서 '당신을 돕게 되어 영광입니다'의 뜻이다:
= <It would be an honor to assist you.>

Fundamental Exercises

1. 다음 문장을 읽고 밑줄 친 부분에 적합한 영어단어를 기입하시오.

I really appreciated your ______________ the file to me. (제게 파일을 보내주셔서 너무 감사했습니다.)

→ ____

2. 다음 내용을 읽고 이에 적합한 영어문장을 고르시오.

저를 취업면접에 초대해 주셔서 감사합니다.

① I thank you for invite me to the job interview.
② I am really thankful of your inviting me to the job interview.
③ I really appreciate your inviting me to the job interview.
④ I am really appreciate your invitation me to the job interview.

3. 다음 문장을 영작하시오.

제 숙제를 도와주셔서 감사합니다.

→ ____

4. 다음 밑줄 친 전치사구(prepositional phrase)에 해당하는 내용을 <during>을 활용하여 영작하시오.

Once again, I thank you for your consideration of me ____________________. (당신의 공장을 방문하는 동안, 저에 대한 당신의 배려에 다시 한 번 감사드립니다.)

→ ____

5. 다음 문장을 올바르게 수정하여 전체 문장을 다시 쓰시오.

Would there be something you may need from me, please feel freely to contact me at any time. (제게 필요한 것이 있으시면, 편하게 언제든지 연락주십시오.)

→ ____

____

10장

영문 비즈니스 이메일Ⅲ - 사과 이메일

사과이메일은 자신의 잘못으로 인해 화가 난 사람에게 보내는 서신이기 때문에 구구절절 변명을 늘어놓기보다는 자신의 실수를 겸허한 자세로 수용하면서 해결방안에 대해 명확하게 제시하는 것이 좋다. 만약 전적으로 자신의 잘못이 아니라고 해도 이에 대해 책임을 지는 자세가 필요하며 조금이라도 자신의 잘못이 있는 경우에는 이를 받아들이고 개선하고자 하는 의지를 보여야 한다. 직장 생활을 하면서 자신의 과실로 인해 상대방에게 손해나 불편을 끼치는 경우가 생길 수 있다. 비즈니스 관계에서의 사과는 단순히 사과 그 자체에 그치는 것이 아니라 경우에 따라 시정조치를 취하거나 상대방에게 보상을 약속해야 하는 경우가 많은데, 이 경우에는 구체적인 해결방안 또는 보상방안을 제시하는 것이 바람직하다. 영문으로 사과 이메일을 보낼 때 정해진 서론 표현이 있는 것은 아니지만 이에 해당하는 일반적인 패턴으로는 <~에 대해 사과하다>가 있다.

I apologize for ~ **I am sorry for ~** **Please accept my apologies for ~**[51]	~ 에 대해 사과하다

---

51) **Examples**:

→ I **apologize for** misplacing the file.

I'm **sorry for** misplacing the file.

Please **accept** my **apology for** having misplaced the file.

I'm **sorry that** I misplaced the file.

My **apologies to** Gerald **for** misplacing the file.

Please **give** my **apologies to** Gerald **for** misplacing the file.

Exercises:

귀사의 주문을 오늘 오전까지 납품하지 못한 것에 대해 사과드립니다.

→ ____

<supplying / your order>

당신이 전화로 요청한 카탈로그를 보내지 못한 것에 대해 사과드립니다.

→ ____

<requested / on>

저희와 함께 근무했던 Smith 씨에 대한 정보를 제공하지 못한 것에 대해 사과드립니다.

→ ____

<provide A with B / about / Mr. / who>

Answers:

귀사의 주문을 오늘 오전까지 납품하지 못한 것에 대해 사과드립니다.

<supplying / your order>

→ I **apologize for** not supplying your order by this morning.

≠ I apologize **to you** for not supplying your order by this morning. (Δ)

* <apologize>와 <for> 사이에 <to you>를 붙이면 어색한 문장이 된다.

= **I am sorry for** not supplying your order by this morning.

≠ I am sorry for not **my** supplying your order by this morning. (X)

* <not>와 <supplying> 사이에 <my>를 붙이면 틀린 문장이 된다.

= **Please accept my apologies for** not supplying your order by this morning.

≠ Please accept my apologies for not **my** supplying your order by this morning. (X)

* <not>와 <supplying> 사이에 <my>를 붙이면 틀린 문장이 된다.

= **My appologies** (to you) **for** not supplying your order by this morning.

당신이 전화로 요청한 카탈로그를 보내지 못한 것에 대해 사과드립니다.

<requested / on>

→ I **apologize for** not sending the catalogues, which you requested on the phone.

= I apologize for not sending the catalogues, which you requested **by** the phone.

= I apologize for not sending the catalogues, which you requested **through** the phone.

* <catalogues> 뒤에 <to you>를 붙이지 않는 것이 좋다.

* 상대방이 catalogues 다시 말해 전화로 요청한 catalogues라는 것에 대해 이미 알고 있는 상황에서는 관계대명사(which) 앞에 쉼표를 붙인다.

→ 관계대명사의 계속적 용법: 부연설명의 역할

= **I am sorry for** not sending the catalogues, which you requested on the phone.
= **Please accept my apologies for** not sending the catalogues, which you requested on the phone.
= **My appologies** (to you) **for** not sending the catalogues, which you requested on the phone.

저희와 함께 근무했던 Smith 씨에 대한 정보를 제공하지 못한 것에 대해 사과드립니다.

<provide A with B / about / Mr. / who>

→ **I apologize for** not providing you with the information **about** Mr. Smith, who worked with us.

* 위 문장에서 <about> 대신에 <in regards to>나 <regarding>을 사용할 수 있지만 <considering>의 경우에는 사용할 수 없다.

= I apologize for not providing you with the information **in regards to** Mr. Smith, who worked with us. (O)
= I apologize for not providing you with the information **regarding** Mr. Smith, who worked with us. (O)
≠ I apologize for not providing you with the information **considering** Mr. Smith, who worked with us. (X)

* 위 문장에서 전치사 <on>을 쓰는 경우에는 다음과 같이 문장을 변경해야 한다:

I apologize for not providing you with the information **on the subject of** Mr Smith, who worked with us. (Δ)

* 상대방이 Mr. Smith에 대해 이미 알고 있는 경우에는 관계대명사(who) 앞에 쉼표를 붙인다.

→ 관계대명사의 계속적 용법: 부연설명의 역할

= **I am sorry for** not providing you with the information on Mr. Smith, who worked with us.
= **Please accept my apologies for** not providing you with the information on Mr. Smith, who worked with us.
= **My appologies** (to you) **for** not providing you with the information on Mr. Smith, who worked with us.

Part 1 Example of a Business Email: Apology Email

** 다음 사과 이메일은 지나친 변명조의 글로서 구체적인 해결방안을 제시하지 못한다는 점에서 바람직하지 못한 이메일의 사례라고 할 수 있다.

사과 이메일

제목: 비행기를 놓쳐서 죄송합니다.

박과장님께

오늘 중국행 비행기를 놓친 점에 대해서 진심으로 사과드립니다. 솔직히 말씀드리면, 공항으로 가는 길에 차가 많이 막혔습니다. 탑승구에 도착해서 직원에게 들여보내 달라고 애원해보았지만, 그 직원은 제 말을 듣지 않았습니다.

유감스럽게도, 다음 항공편은 내일 오후에 있습니다. 중국에서 있을 매우 중요한 회의에 참석하지 못하게 되어 과장님께서 매우 화가 나셨으리라 생각합니다. 그래도 저를 여전히 믿어 주시기를 바라는 마음입니다. 제가 이 실수를 만회하기 위해서 할 수 있는 모든 노력을 기울일 것이라는 것을 약속드립니다. 제 커다란 실수를 용서해 주십시오. 여기에서나마 China Project를 지원하기 위해 최선을 다하겠습니다.

이러한 실수는 앞으로 없을 겁니다. 다시 사과드립니다.

안녕히 계십시오.

Brad Finnie

<English Words and Idioms>

apologize for ~에 대해 사과하다
miss 놓치다
flight 항공편
traffic 교통량
on the way 가는 길에 (도중에)

<examples>: It is **on the way** to the station. (그것은 역으로 가는 길에 있어요)
I listen to the radio **on the way** to work. (저는 출근길에 라디오를 들어요)

reach 도착하다
beg 애원하다
staff 직원

unfortunately 유감스럽게도
miss 참석하지 못하다
extremely 매우
angry at ~에게 화가 나다
trust 믿다, 신뢰하다
do everything 모든 노력을 기울이다
make it up to you 보상하다 (갚다) → '실수를 만회하다'라는 우회적인 의미
try one's best 최선을 다하다
assist with ~을 돕다

Part 2 영작연습

다음 문장을 영작하시오.

사과 이메일

→ ______________________________

제목: 비행기를 놓쳐서 죄송합니다.

→ ______________________________

<my apologies for>

박과장님께

→ __________________________

1. The First Paragraph

오늘 중국행 비행기를 놓친 점에 대해서 진심으로 사과드립니다.

→ ____

<apologize for / to>

솔직히 말씀드리면, 공항으로 가는 길에 차가 많이 막혔습니다.

→ ____

<frankly / there was / traffic / on the way>

탑승구에 도착해서 직원에게 들여보내 달라고 애원해보았지만, 그 직원은 제 말을 듣지 않았습니다.

→ ____

<when / reach / beg / staff / let me in>

2. The Second Paragraph

유감스럽게도, 다음 항공편은 내일 오후에 있습니다.

→ ______________________________

<unfortunately>

중국에서 있을 매우 중요한 회의에 참석하지 못하게 되어 과장님께서 매우 화가 나셨으리라 생각합니다.

→ ______________________________

____

<know / missed / extremely / so / angry at>

그래도 저를 여전히 믿어 주시기를 바라는 마음입니다.

→ ______________________________

<however / hope / can>

제가 이 실수를 만회하기 위해서 할 수 있는 모든 노력을 기울일 것이라는 것을 약속드립니다.

→ ______________________________

<do everything / make it up to you>

제 커다란 실수를 용서해 주십시오.

→ ______________________________

<huge>

여기에서나마 China Project를 지원하기 위해 최선을 다하겠습니다.

→ ______________________________

<try my best / assist with / even>

3. The Third Paragraph

이러한 실수는 앞으로 없을 겁니다.

→ ______________________________

<happen>

다시 사과드립니다.

→ ______________________________

<apologize to>

안녕히 계십시오.

→ ________________

Brad Finnie

Part 3 정답과 해설

사과 이메일
→ Apology Email

제목: 비행기를 놓쳐서 죄송합니다.
→ Subject: My Apologies for Missing the Flight (O)
≠ Subject: My Apologies for Missing the **Airplane (X)**

**** 원어민 설명: airplane**(비행기)과 **flight**(항공편) 차이:
The airplane is actually the plane, itself. Flight is the route that the airplane takes, or the journey that the airplane takes. When you say that you missed the flight, it means that you missed the scheduled journey of the airplane.

박과장님께
→ Dear Manager Park,

1. The First Paragraph

오늘 중국행 비행기를 놓친 점에 대해서 진심으로 사과드립니다.
<apologize for / to>
→ I apologize for missing the flight to China today.

솔직히 말씀드리면, 공항으로 가는 길에 차가 많이 막혔습니다.
<frankly / there was / traffic / on the way>
→ Frankly, there was **a lot of** traffic on the way to the airport.
≠ Frankly, there was **many** traffic on the way to the airport. (X)

* <traffic>은 불가산명사기 때문에 앞에 'much' 나 'a lot of'가 올 수 있지만 'many'는 올 수 없다.

탑승구에 도착해서 직원에게 들여보내 달라고 애원해보았지만, 그 직원은제 말을 듣지 않았습니다.
<when / reach / beg / staff / let me in>
→ When I **reached** the gate, I begged the staff to let me in, but **he** didn't listen to me.
= When I **arrived at** the gate, I begged the staff to let me in, but **he** didn't listen to me.

* 직원이 남성인 경우 대명사 **he**를 쓰고 이와 반대로 여성인 경우에는 **she**를 쓴다.

2. The Second Paragraph

유감스럽게도, 다음 항공편은 내일 오후에 있습니다.

<unfortunately>

→ Unfortunately, the next flight will be tomorrow afternoon.

≠ Unfortunately, the next **airplane** will be tomorrow afternoon. **(X)**

중국에서 있을 매우 중요한 회의에 참석하지 못하게 되어 과장님께서 매우 화가 나셨으리라 생각합니다.

<know / missed / extremely / so / angry at>

→ (I know) I missed an extremely important meeting in China, so I think you are too angry at me.

그래도 저를 여전히 믿어 주시기를 바라는 마음입니다.

<however / hope / can>

→ However, I hope that you can still **trust** me. **(O)**

However, I hope that you can still **believe** me. **(X)**

* <**believe me**>는 '내 말이나 행동을 믿어 달라'는 뜻이고, <**trust me**>는 "나'라는 사람 자체를 믿어 달라'는 뜻이기 때문에 이 문맥에서는 <trust>를 써야 한다.

제가 이 실수를 만회하기 위해서 할 수 있는 모든 노력을 기울일 것이라는 것을 약속드립니다.

<do everything / make it up to you>

→ I promise to do everything I can to make it up to you.

≠ I promise to do everything **which (that)** I can to make it up to you. **(X)**

* 위 문맥에서 <everything> 뒤에 관계대명사(which, that)를 적으면 틀린 문장이 된다:

* 위 문맥에서 <I can>을 생략해도 동일한 의미의 올바른 문장이 된다:

→ I promise to do everything to make it up to you.

* <make it up to you>를 직역하면 '당신에게 손해가 갔으니 보상하겠습니다.'라는 <pay you back>의 뜻이다. 자신이 실수를 하여 상대방에게 피해를 주게 되는 상황에서 사용할 수 있는 표현으로서 '실수를 만회하다'라는 우회적인 의미로 보면 된다.

제 커다란 실수를 용서해 주십시오.

<huge>

→ Please forgive my huge mistake.

여기에서나마 China Project를 지원하기 위해 최선을 다하겠습니다.
<try my best / assist with / even>

→ I will try my best to **assist with** the China Project even from here. **(O)**
≠ I will try my best to **assist** the China Project even from here. **(X)**

* <assist> 뒤에 사물이 오면 전치사 'with'를 붙여야 한다. 반대로 <assist> 뒤에 사람이 오는 경우에는 전치사 없이 바로 목적어(사람)가 온다: (Ex) I assisted my younger brother.

3. The Third Paragraph

이러한 실수는 앞으로 없을 겁니다.
<happen>

→ Such a mistake will not happen.

다시 사과드립니다.
<apologize to>

→ Again, I apologize to you.

안녕히 계십시오.
→ Sincerely,

Brad Finnie

Part 4 Final Draft

Apology Email

Subject: My Apologies for Missing the Flight

Dear Manager Park:

I apologize for missing the flight to China today. Frankly, there was a lot of traffic on the way to the airport. When I reached the gate, I begged the staff to let me in, but he didn't listen to me.

Unfortunately, the next flight will be tomorrow afternoon. I know I missed an extremely important meeting in China, so I think you are too angry at me. However, I hope that you can still trust me. I promise to do everything I can to make it up to you. Please forgive my huge mistake. I will try my best to assist with the China Project even from here.

Such a mistake will not happen. Again, I apologize to you.

Sincerely,

Brad Finnie

Part 5 Native English Speaker's Revision for the Final Draft

** 다음 사과 이메일은 자신의 실수를 수용하면서 이에 대한 해결방법을 보다 적극적으로 제시한다는 점에서 바람직한 이메일의 사례라고 할 수 있다.

사과 이메일

제목: 비행기를 놓친 것과 관련하여

박과장님께

오늘 중국행 비행기를 놓친 것에 대해 사과드립니다. 솔직히 말씀드리면, 공항으로 가는 길에 교통체증이 너무 심해서 제가 제 시간에 탑승구에 도착하지 못했습니다.

제가 너무나도 중요한 회의에 참석하지 못한 것에 대해 정말 너무 죄송하고 몹시 실망스럽습니다. 그것이 과장님과 우리 비즈니스에 얼마나 큰 의미인지 알고 있습니다. 따라서 회의일정을 다시 잡아서 제가 맡은 일을 완수하도록 최선을 다하겠습니다.

제가 China Project의 적임자라는 것을 여전히 믿어 주시기를 바랍니다. 부디 제가 실수를 만회할 수 있도록 허락해주십시오. 바라던 결과를 반드시 성공시켜서 전해드리겠습니다.

Truly Yours,

김나윤

<English Words and Idioms>

regarding ~과 관련하여
massive 심각한 (엄청나게 큰)
traffic jam 교통체증
prevent A from B A가 B하지 못하게 하다
make it to ~에 도착하다
in time 제 시간에

deeply 몹시, 매우
disappointed 실망스러운
therefore 따라서
try one's best 최선을 다하다
reschedule 일정을 다시 잡다
accomplish 완수하다 (완성하다)
assignment 맡은 일 (임무)

have confidence in someone ~를 믿다
right person for ~의 적임자
be determinded to 반드시 ~하다 (~하기로 결심하다)
desired 바라던 (희망하던)

Part 6 영작연습

다음 문장을 영작하시오.

사과 이메일

→ ______________________

제목: 비행기를 놓친 것과 관련하여

→ ________________________________

<regarding>

박과장님께

→ _____________________

<Manager>

1. The First Paragraph

오늘 중국행 비행기를 놓친 것에 대해 사과드립니다.

→ ____

<apologize for>

솔직히 말씀드리면, 공항으로 가는 길에 교통체증이 너무 심해서, 제가 제 시간에 탑승구에 도착하지 못했습니다.

→ ____

____

<frankly / massive / traffic jam / prevent A from B / making it to / in time>

2. The Second Paragraph

제가 너무나도 중요한 회의에 참석하지 못한 것에 대해 정말 너무 죄송하고 몹시 실망스럽습니다.

→ ____

<really / sorry / deeply / missed / very>

그것이 과장님과 우리 비즈니스에 얼마나 큰 의미인지 알고 있습니다.

→ ____

<how much>

따라서 회의일정을 다시 잡아서 제가 맡은 일을 완수하도록 최선을 다하겠습니다.

→ ____

<therefore / reschedule / accomplish / assignment>

3. The Third Paragraph

제가 China Project의 적임자라는 것을 여전히 믿어 주시기를 바랍니다.

→ ____

<hope / will still have confidence in someone / to / right person for>

부디 제가 실수를 만회할 수 있도록 허락해주십시오.

→ ____

<allow A to ~ / make it up to you>

바라던 결과를 반드시 성공시켜서 전해드리겠습니다.

→ ____

<be determined to / desired result>

Truly Yours,

김나윤

→ ____________________

Part 7 정답과 해설

사과 이메일
→ Apology Email

제목: 비행기를 놓친 것과 관련하여
<regarding>
→ Subject: Regarding Missing the Flight
= Subject: Regarding **the Missed** Flight

박과장님께
<Manager>
→ Dear Manager Park,

1. The First Paragraph

오늘 중국행 비행기를 놓친 것에 대해 사과드립니다.
<apologize for>
→ I apologize for missing the flight to China today.

솔직히 말씀드리면, 공항으로 가는 길에 교통체증이 너무 심해서, 제가 제 시간에 탑승구에 도착하지 못했습니다.
<frankly / massive / traffic jam / prevent A from B / making it to / in time>
→ Frankly, there was a massive traffic jam on the way to the airport, preventing me from making it to the gate in time.
* <traffic jam>은 가산명사기 때문에 앞에 관사 a를 붙인다

= Frankly, there was a massive traffic jam on the way to the airport **that (which) prevented** me **from** making it to the gate in time.
= Frankly, there was a massive traffic jam on the way to the traffic jam, **therefore** I could not **arrive at** the gate in time.
* 위 문장에서 <therefore> 대신에 <so>를 쓰면 비격식체 문장이 된다.

** **보충설명:** 교통체증 (traffic jam = traffic congestion, bumper-to-bumper traffic)
교통량 (traffic)
* <a massive traffic jam>은 <a lot of traffic> 혹은 <much traffic>과 바꾸어 쓸 수 있다.

2. The Second Paragraph

제가 너무나도 중요한 회의에 참석하지 못한 것에 대해 정말 너무 죄송하고 몹시 실망스럽습니다.
<really / sorry / deeply / missed / very>
→ I am really very sorry and deeply disappointed that I missed a very important meeting.

그것이 과장님과 우리 비즈니스에 얼마나 큰 의미인지 알고 있습니다.
<how much>
→ I know how much it means to you and to our business.
= I know how much it means to you **and our** business.

따라서 회의일정을 다시 잡아서 제가 맡은 일을 완수하도록 최선을 다하겠습니다.
<therefore / reschedule / accomplish / assignment>
→ Therefore, I will try my best to reschedule the meeting and to accomplish my assignment.
= Therefore, I will try my best to reschedule the meeting **and accomplish** my assignment.

3. The Third Paragraph

제가 China Project의 적임자라는 것을 여전히 믿어 주시기를 바랍니다.
<hope / will still have confidence in someone / to / right person for>
→ I hope that you will still have confidence in me to be the right person for the China Project.

부디 제가 실수를 만회할 수 있도록 허락해주십시오.
<allow A to ~ / make it up to you>
→ Please allow me to make it up to you.
* **<make it up to you>**는 '실수를 만회하다'라는 우회적인 의미로서 자신의 실수를 인정하면서 상사의 기분을 풀어줄 때 사용할 수 있는 표현이다.

바라던 결과를 반드시 성공시켜서 전해드리겠습니다.
<be determined to / desired result>
→ I am determined to succeed and to deliver the desired result.
= I am determined to succeed **and deliver** the desired result.

Truly Yours,

김나윤
→ Nayoon Kim

Part 8 Final Draft

Aplogy Email

Subject: Regarding Missing the Flight

Dear Manager Park,

I apologize for missing the flight to China today. Frankly, there was a massive traffic jam on the way to the airport, preventing me from making it to the gate in time.

I am really very sorry and deeply disappointed that I missed a very important meeting. I know how much it means to you and our business. Therefore, I will try my best to reschedule the meeting and accomplish my assignment.

I hope that you will still have confidence in me to be the right person for the China Project. Please allow me to make it up to you. I am determined to succeed and deliver the desired result.

Truly yours,

Nayoon Kim

Fundamental Exercises

1. 다음 문장을 읽고 빈 칸에 들어갈 올바른 구문을 고르시오.

I apologize ________________ your order by this morning.
(귀사의 주문을 오늘 오전까지 납품하지 못한 것에 대해 사과드립니다.)

① for not my supplying
② not for supplying
③ for not supplying
④ not for my supplying

2. 다음 밑줄 친 곳에 적합한, 모든 가능한 전치사를 적으시오.

I apologize for not providing you with the information ________ Mr. Smith, who worked with us.
(저희와 함께 근무했던 Mr. Smith에 대한 정보를 제공하지 못한 것에 대해 사과드립니다.)

→ ______________________________

3. 다음 문장을 읽고 밑줄 친 곳에 적합한 수량형용사와 전치사를 적으시오.

Frankly, there was _______________ traffic _________ the way to the airport.
(솔직히 말씀드리면, 공항으로 가는 길에 차가 많이 막혔습니다.)

→ ______________________________

4. 다음 문장을 읽고 틀린 부분을 수정하여 전체 문장을 다시 쓰시오.

However, I hope that you can still believe me.
(그래도 저를 여전히 믿어 주시기를 바라는 마음입니다.)

→ ______________________________

5. 다음 문장을 영작하시오.

제가 이 실수를 만회하기 위해서 할 수 있는 모든 노력을 기울일 것이라는 것을 약속드립니다.

→ ______________________________

11장

영문 비즈니스 팩스 Ⅰ

fax(팩스)는 facsimile(팩시밀리)의 줄임말로서 전기통신선을 이용하여 문서의 복사본을 전송하는 통신수단이다. 예전에 비해 팩스의 사용 빈도수가 줄어들었다고는 하지만 아직도 기업 간에는 영수증이나 간단한 서신, 송장, 견적서 등과 같은 문서를 팩스를 통해 확인하고 있다. 최근에는 인터넷을 통한 eFax(인터넷 팩스)의 등장으로 팩스기가 아닌 PC를 활용하여 보다 손쉽게 문서를 확인하고 나아가 비용까지 절감하는 효과를 거두고 있다. 일반적으로 팩스는 문서나 이메일보다 짧고 간결한 특징을 가지며 수신자만 팩스내용을 본다는 보장이 없기 때문에 다른 문서 전송 방식에 비해 기밀성이 떨어지는 한계를 갖기도 한다. 그러나 팩스는 이메일과 달리 사용자 개인의 암호가 없어도 누구나 팩스를 받아 볼 수 있는 신속성과 편리함으로 업무시간을 단축시킬 수 있다는 장점을 지닌다.

Part 1 Format of a Business Fax Cover Sheet

앞서 언급한 것처럼, 공용으로 사용하는 팩스는 누구나 볼 수 있기 때문에 일반적으로 팩스를 보낼 때 팩스표지(fax cover sheet)를 포함시키는 것이 좋다. 팩스를 전송하는 과정에서 팩스표지가 절대적으로 필요한 것은 아니지만 특히 팩스를 처음 보내거나 팩스 내용 자체가 민감한 사안을 다루는 경우에는 팩스표지를 쓰는 것이 좋다. 팩스표지에는 다음과 같이 수신자 이름, 수신자 팩스번호, 수신자 전화번호, 페이지 수 그리고 제목을 적는다.

TO:	수신자 이름
FAX #:	수신자 팩스번호
PHONE #:	수신자 전화번호
NO. PAGES:	페이지 수
SUBJECT:	제목

Part 2 Format of a Business Fax

Company's letterhead[52] information (헤더)

(logo, company name, address of company, and contact information, such as phone number, email address, or website) - 회사로고, 이름, 주소, 연락처

Fax

From: (발신자 이름 및 직위[53]) - 경우에 따라 발신자의 직위도 기재할 수 있다.
Fax: (발신자 팩스번호) - 팩스번호는 지역번호까지 기재한다.
Phone: (발신자 전화번호)
Date: (발신 날짜) - 년, 월일 모두 기입한다.

To: (수신자 이름 및 직위[54])
Fax: (수신자 팩스번호)
Phone: (수신자 전화번호)
No. Pages: (페이지 수) - 팩스 문서가 여러 장일 때 페이지 누락 방지를 위해 페이지 수를 기재한다.

Subject: (제목)

Salutation: (인사말) - 인사말, 본문, 끝인사와 서명 등은 비즈니스 레터/이메일 작성방식과 동일하다.

Message (본문내용)

Closing, (끝인사)

Signature (서명)
Name of Sender (발신자 이름)

And possibly additional pages for the fax. (추가되는 페이지 있을 수 있음)

** 보충설명: 비즈니스 팩스 표기방식

① Fax and Telephone Number 표기법

팩스번호와 전화번호를 기재할 때 번호 중간에 dash (-)를 사용하여 보기 쉽도록 만든다.

fax: **212**-454-1234 (**지역번호** – 팩스번호)

phone: **604**-123-4455 (**지역번호** – 전화번호)

② Date 표기법

년도와 월일 모두 기입한다: 월 날짜, 년도

March 15, 2020

* 날짜표기와 관련하여, <월/날짜/년도> 와 <날짜/달/년도>는 비격식체 표기로 간주된다:

Examples: 3/15/2020 (△)
15/03/2020 (△)

③ No. Pages 표기법

팩스 문서에 페이지 수를 기입함으로써 중간에 누락 되는 페이지가 없도록 한다. 팩스를 처음 보내는 경우에는 팩스표지까지 포함한 전체 페이지 수를 기재한다. 이때 팩스표지를 포함하여 두 장인 경우에는 "2 (inclusive of the fax cover)"라고 적고, 팩스표지 없이 두 장인 경우에는 "2"로 표기하면 된다. 또한 팩스표지 없이 한 장인 경우에는 "1"으로 표기하면 된다.

④ Subject 표기법

제목과 관련하여, 두 번째 단어의 첫 레터를 대문자로 사용할지 소문자로 사용할지는 개인의 선택이다. 예를 들어 짧은 제목인 경우에는 대문자로 그리고 긴 제목인 경우에는 소문자로 쓰는 것이 좋다.

Examples:

Subject (짧은 제목일 때): **R**oom **R**eservation (O)
Room reservation (△)

Subject (긴 제목일 때) : **D**ecision on **n**ew **p**roduct **d**etails[55] (O)
Decision on **N**ew **P**roduct **D**etails (△)

⑤ Closing 표기법

팩스에서 끝인사는 비즈니스레터나 이메일에서 사용되는 끝인사 작성방식과 동일하다. 그러나 영수증이나 견적서를 팩스로 보낼 때에는 끝인사를 주로 생략한다.

---

52) 'letterhead'는 편지지 윗부분에 인쇄된 (회사 로고와 더불어) 발신자의 이름, 회사 이름, 주소, 연락처 등을 의미하는데 간혹 'header'로도 쓰인다.

53) Example: Derek Jones, Data Management Representative (데이터 관리자) - optional

54) Example: Louise Smith, Human Resources Representative (인사(부) 책임자)

55) product details (제품설명서)

Part 3 Example of a Business Fax

Global Travel Agency
281 Lincoln Rd. New York NY, 40125
Phone: 585-123-4455 Fax: 585-123-4457
Website: www. globaltravel.com

팩스

발신자 이름 및 직위: Claire Park, Global Travel Agency 이사
발신자 팩스번호: 585-123-4457
발신자 전화번호: 585-123-4455
발신 날짜: 2022년 3월 15일

수신자 이름 및 직위: Louise Smith 씨, Sunny Hotel 과장
수신자 팩스번호: 585-914-1234
수신자 전화번호: 585-914-1237
페이지 수: 1

제목: 객실 예약

Louise Smith 씨에게

저희 여행사는 6월 9일에서 14일까지 6박 동안 더블룸 25실을 예약하고 싶습니다. 가능한 빨리, 객실의 이용가능성과 견적을 확인해주시면 감사하겠습니다.

Sincerely yours,

Claire Park

Claire Park

<English Words and Idioms>

reservation 예약
travel agency 여행사
make reservations 예약하다
inclusive 포함된 (언급된 날짜, 월, 수 등을 포함하여 ~부터 ~까지)
appreciate 고맙게 생각하다
confirmation 확인
availability 이용가능성
quote 견적
as soon as possible 가능한 빨리

Part 4 영작연습

다음 문장을 영작하시오.

팩스

→ ____________________

발신자 이름 및 직위: Claire Park, Global Travel Agency 이사

→ ____________________

발신자 팩스번호: 585-123-4457

→ ____________________

발신자 전화번호: 585-123-4455

→ ____________________

발신 날짜: 2022년 3월 15일

→ ____________________

수신자 이름 및 직위: Louise Smith씨, Sunny Hotel 과장

→ ____________________

수신자 팩스번호: 585-914-1234

→ ____________________

수신자 전화번호: 585-914-1237

→ ____________________

페이지 수: 1

→ ____________________

제목: 객실예약

→ ____________

Louise Smith 씨에게

→ __________________

저희 여행사는 6월 9일에서 14일까지 6박 동안 더블룸 25실을 예약하고 싶습니다.

→ ____

<would like to / make reservations for / inclusive>

가능한 빨리, 객실의 이용가능성과 견적을 확인해주시면 감사하겠습니다.

→ ____

<would appreciate / confirmation / availability / quote>

Sincerely yours,

Claire Park

Claire Park

Part 5 정답과 해설

팩스
→ **Fax**

발신자 이름 및 직위: Claire Park, Global Travel Agency 이사
→ From: Claire Park, Director **of** Global Travel Agency
* 위 문맥에서 전치사 of를 제외한 다른 전치사를 사용하면 틀린 문장이 된다.

발신자 팩스번호: 585-123-4457
→ Fax: 585-123-4457
발신자 전화번호: 585-123-4455
→ Phone: 585-123-4455
발신 날짜: 2022년 3월 15일
→ Date: March 15, 2022

수신자 이름 및 직위: Louise Smith 씨, Sunny Hotel 과장
→ To: Ms. Louise Smith, Manager of Sunny Hotel
수신자 팩스번호: 585-914-1234
→ Fax: 585-914-1234
수신자 전화번호: 585-914-1237
→ Phone: 585-914-1237
페이지 수: 1
→ No. Pages: 1

제목: 객실 예약
→ Subject: Room Reservation

Louise Smith 씨에게
→ Dear Ms. Louise Smith,

저희 여행사는 6월 9일에서 14일까지 6박 동안 더블룸 25실을 예약하고 싶습니다.
<would like to / make reservations for / inclusive>

→ Our travel agency would like to make reservations for twenty five double rooms for six nights from June 9 to 14 **inclusive.**

= Our travel agency would like to make reservations for twenty five double rooms for six nights from June 9 to 14 **inclusive, for a departure date of June 15.**

* 'inclusive'[56] 다음에 쉼표(,)를 적고 'for a departure date of June 15' 구문을 붙이는 것은 14일 날 퇴실(check out)하는 것이 아니라 14일도 숙박일수에 포함된다는 것, 다시 말해 출발일자가 6월 15일이라는 것을 명백하게 알리기 위해서이다. 이때 'inclusive' 다음에 전치사 'for'를 붙인다.

= Our travel agency would like to make a reservation for twenty five double rooms for six nights from June 9 to 14 **inclusive. We would like a departure date of June 15.**

가능한 빨리, 객실의 이용가능성과 견적을 확인해주시면 감사하겠습니다.
<would appreciate / confirmation / availability / quote>

→ I **would** appreciate confirmation of the availability of the rooms and a quote as soon as possible. (OO)

* 위 문장에서 <would> 대신 <will>을 쓰면 틀린 문장이 된다.

= I **would** appreciate it if you **could send** me your offer regarding the price. Also, as soon as you can, please confirm if there are enough rooms available for us to use during that time period. (O)

* 비즈니스 영문 팩스는 간결체로 보내야 하기 때문에 이 문장보다 위의 문장이 더 바람직한 표현이라고 할 수 있다.

Sincerely yours,

Claire Park

Claire Park

56) **<inclusive>가 삽입된 다른 예문과 설명**: You have 5 kids in a line up. John, Derek, Olivia, Emily, and Edmund, in a single file. The line needs to separate at Olivia, inclusive. This means that John, Derek, and Olivia need to be separated from Emily and Edmund. → **If you say that** the line should separate at Olivia, it is not clear if Olivia should be separated as well, or just John and Derek, which is why you might add the word. 'inclusive'.

Part 6 Final Draft

Global Travel Agency
281 Lincoln Rd.[57] New York NY, 40125[58]
Phone: 585-123-4455 Fax: 585-123-4457
Website: www. globaltravel.com

Fax

From: Claire Park, Director of Global Travel Agency
Fax: 585-123-4457
Phone: 585-123-4455
Date: March 15, 2022

To: Ms. Louise Smith, Manager of Sunny Hotel
Fax: 585-914-1234
Phone: 585-914-1237
No. Pages: 1

Subject: Room Reservation

Dear Ms. Louise Smith,

Our travel agency would like to make reservations for twenty five double rooms for six nights from June 9 to 14 inclusive. I would appreciate confirmation of the availability of the rooms and a quote as soon as possible.

Sincerely yours,

Claire Park

Claire Park
Global Travel Agency

57) Road의 줄임말로서 Rd뒤에 마침표(.)를 붙인다.
* 도로명(street name) 약어의 예시: Rd. = Road
Ave. = Avenue
St. = Street
Wy. = Way
Hwy. = Highway

58) 번지, 도로명, 도시명, 주이름, 우편번호

** 보충설명: 주소표기 방식

① 편지 및 팩스 작성을 위한 주소 표기방식:

정해진 주소 표기방식은 없으나 현재 북미에서 보편적으로 활용되고 있는 방식은 주이름과 우편번호 사이에만 쉼표를 붙인다.

Example: 110 S Garfield St.
Mount Angel OR, 97345
USA

② 편지 봉투 작성을 위한 주소 표기방식:

주이름과 우편번호 사이에 쉼표를 붙이지 않는다.

Example: 110 S Garfield St.
Mount Angel OR 97345
USA

<영수증 실제 샘플>

café
Britt
www.cafebritt.com

Bill to:	Ship to:
jae kim 575 main street 1313 ny NY 10044 US	Jae Kim 575 main street 1313 ny NY 10044 US

Account No.	Order Date	Invoice No.
	04/08/2016	96-523572

Credit Card	Telephone
xxxx-xxxx-xxxx-4606	6464839863

Quantity	Description	Price/Item	Total
1.00	ORGANIC SHADE GROWN GOURMET COFFEE FROM CAFE BRITT	13.95	$13.95
1.00	COSTA RICAN DARK ROAST GOURMET COFFEE FROM CAFE BRITT	12.95	$12.95
1.00	COSTA RICAN TARRAZU MONTECIELO GOURMET COFFEE FROM CAF	12.95	$12.95
	Subtotal:	$ 39.85	
	Shipping and Handling	$9.50	
	Tax	$ 0.00	
	Total	**$49.35**	

ME-F-04

Page 1 of 1

FROM THE PLANTATION TO YOUR CUP!

Café Britt Satisfaction Guaranteed
Thank you for choosing Café Britt as your gourmet coffee company.

info@cafebritt.com
1-800-GO-BRITT
(1-800-462-7488)
Fax: 1-800-652-5679
2960 NW 72nd Ave.
Miami, Fl, 33122

Shop on line at
www.cafebritt.com

Fundamental Exercises

1. <fax cover sheet>에 포함되지 않는 것을 고르시오.

① Recipient name ② Reference ③ No. Pages ④ Subject

2. <No. Pages> 표기법과 관련하여, 팩스 겉장을 포함하여 세 장인 경우 이를 어떻게 작성하는가?

① This page + 2
② 3
③ 3 (inclusive of the fax cover)
④ three pages

3. 다음 내용을 읽고 이에 적합한 영어문장을 고르시오.

저희 여행사는 6월 9일에서 14일까지 6박 동안 더블룸 25실을 예약하고 싶습니다.

① Our travel agent would like to make reservations about twenty five single rooms for six night from June 9 to 14.
② Our travel agency would like to make reservation for twenty five double room for six nights from June 9 to 14 inclusive.
③ Our travel agency would like to make reservations for twenty five double rooms for six nights from June 9 to 14 inclusive.
④ Our travel agent would like to make a reservation to twenty five double rooms for six nights from June 9 to 14 inclusive.

4. 다음 문장을 올바르게 수정하여 전체 문장을 다시 쓰시오.

I will appreciate confirmation of the available of the rooms and a quote as soon as possible. (가능한 빨리, 객실의 이용가능성과 견적을 확인해주시면 감사하겠습니다.)

→ ______________________________

____

5. 팩스번호를 표기할 때 팩스번호 앞에 써야 하는 것은 무엇인가?

① telephone number ② country code ③ area code ④ zip code

12장

영문 비즈니스 팩스 - 견적서 Ⅱ

견적서(estimate/quote)는 구매자의 요청에 따라 (판매자가) 물건의 가격과 제반비용을 미리 알려주는 서류이다. 이때 구매자가 견적서를 받고 가격에 만족하여 구매를 결정하면 서명을 하여 회신하면 된다. 참고로 견적서나 송장을 팩스로 보낼 때에는 인사말(salutation)이나 끝인사(closing)를 생략해도 된다.

Part 1 Example of a Business Fax: Estimate

Pineup Corporation
579 Kemmons Drive Louisville KY, 13567
Phone: 585-123-4455 Fax: 585-123-4457
Website: www. pineupcorporation.com

팩스

발신자 이름 및 직위: Carol Burton, Pineup Corporation 이사
발신자 팩스번호: 585-123-4457
발신자 전화번호: 585-123-4455
발신 날짜: 2022년 5월 6일

수신자 이름 및 직위: Sharon Kim 씨, Woori Enterprise 대리
수신자 팩스번호: 585-914-1234
수신자 전화번호: 585-914-1237
페이지 수: 1

제목: 사무용지와 'Especial Stapler'의 견적서

아래 견적서를 확인해주십시오:

물품번호	수량	품목	단가	공급금액
13590	10	Pineup B4 90 gsm 사무용지 (700장)	10달러	100달러
22481	10	회사로고가 있는 Especial Stapler (스테이플러 철심 2000개 포함)	4달러 50센트	45달러
			소계	145달러
			부가가치세율	10퍼센트
			부가가치세	14달러 50센트
			총액	159달러 5센트

최종결재는 이 견적서에 있는 물품들을 제공하기 전에 부과되어질 것입니다. 이 견적서를 수락하신다면, 이곳에 서명하여 585-123-4457로 팩스를 보내주십시오:

Carol Burton

Carol Burton

Pineup Corporation

<English Words and Idioms>

Director 이사
Assistant Manager 대리
estimate (quote = quotation) 견적서
office paper 사무용지

item 물품번호
quantity 수량
description 품목
unit price 단가
line total 공급금액
gsm – gram per square meter (평방미터 당 그램 수) - 종이의 중량 = 종이의 질
sheet (종이) 한 장
staple 스테이플러 철심
subtotal 소계
VAT Rate 부가가치세율
VAT (Value Added Tax) 부가가치세
total 총액

quotation 견적서
goods 물품, 제품
final payment 최종결재
collect 부과하다 (징수하다, 거두어들이다)
provide A with B ~에게 ~을 제공하다.

Part 2 영작연습

다음 문장을 영작하시오.

팩스

→ _____

발신자 이름 및 직위: Carol Burton, Pineup Corporation 이사

→ ______________________________

발신자 팩스번호: 585-123-4457

→ ______________________________

발신자 전화번호: 585-123-4455

→ ______________________________

발신 날짜: 2022년 5월 6일

→ ______________________________

수신자 이름 및 직위: Sharon Kim 씨, Woori Enterprise 대리

→ ______________________________

수신자 팩스번호: 585-914-1234

→ ______________________________

수신자 전화번호: 585-914-1237

→ ______________________________

페이지 수: 1

→ __________

제목: 사무용지와 'Especial Stapler'의 견적서

→ ________________________________

<estimate for / office paper>

아래 견적서를 확인해주십시오:

→ ________________

<check>

물품번호 ______	수량 ______	품목 ______	단가 ______	공급금액 ______
13590	10	Pineup B4 90 gsm 사무용지 ______ (700장) ______	10달러 ______	100달러 ______
22481	10	회사로고가 있는 Especial Stapler ______ ______ (스테이플러 철심 2000개 포함) ______ ______	4달러 50센트 ______	45달러 ______
			소계 ______	145달러 ______
			부가가치세율 ______	10퍼센트 ______
			부가가치세 ______	14달러 50센트 ______
			총액 ______	159달러 5센트 ______

최종결재는 이 견적서에 있는 물품들을 제공하기 전에 부과되어질 것입니다.

→ ____

<final payment / collect / providing A with B / goods / quote>

이 견서를 수락하신다면, 이곳에 서명하여 585-123-4457로 팩스를 보내주십시오:

→ ____

<to accept / fax>

Carol Burton

Carol Burton

Pineup Corporation

Part 3 정답과 해설

팩스
→ **Fax**

발신자 이름 및 직위: Carol Burton, Pineup Corporation 이사
→ From: Carol Burton, Director of Pineup Corporation

발신자 팩스번호: 585-123-4457
→ Fax: 585-123-4457

발신자 전화번호: 585-123-4455
→ Phone: 585-123-4455

발신 날짜: 2022년 5월 6일
→ Date: May 6, 2022

수신자 이름 및 직위: Sharon Kim 씨, Woori Enterprise 대리
→ To: Ms. Sharon Kim, Assistant Manager of Woori Enterprise

수신자 팩스번호: 585-914-1234
→ Fax: 585-914-1234

수신자 전화번호: 585-914-1237
→ Phone: 585-914-1237

페이지 수: 1
→ No. Pages: 1

제목: 사무용지와 'Especial Stapler'의 견적서
<estimate for / office paper>
→ Subject: Estimate for office paper and 'Especial Stapler'

아래 견적서를 확인해주십시오:
<check>
→ Please check this below estimate:
= Please check this **following** estimate:

물품번호 **Item #**	수량 **Quantity**	품목 **Description**	단가 **Unit Price**	공급금액(수량X단가) **Line Total**[59]
13590	10	**Pineup B4 90 gsm**[60] 사무용지 **Office Paper** 700장 **700 sheets**	10달러 **$10.00**	100달러 **$100.00**
22481	10	회사로고가 있는 'Especial Stapler' **'Especial Stapler' with the company logog** 스테이플러 철심 2000개 포함 **with 2,000 staples**	4달러 50센트 **$4.50**	45달러 **$45.00**
			소계[61] **Subtotal**	145달러 **$145.00**
			부가가치세율 VAT Rate	10퍼센트 **10.00%**
			부가가치세 **VAT**	14달러 50센트 **$14.50**
			총액 **Total**	159달러 5센트 **$159.05**

최종결재는 이 견적서에 있는 물품들을 제공하기 전에 부과되어질 것입니다.

<final payment / collect / providing A with B / goods / quote>

→ The final payment will be collected before providing you with the goods in this quote.

이 견적서를 수락하신다면, 이곳에 서명하여 585-123-4457로 팩스를 보내주십시오:

<to accept / fax>

→ To accept this quote, please sign here and fax **me** at 585-123-4457:

* 위 문장에서 <me>를 생략하고자 하는 경우에는 다음과 같이 수정한다.

= To accept this quote, please sign here and **send the fax to** 585-123-4457.

Carol Burton

Carol Burton

Pineup Corporation

** 참고: 견적서 맨 아래에 감사의 뜻을 전하는 <THANK YOU FOR YOUR BUSINESS> (저희 회사와 거래해 주셔서 감사합니다)를 기입하는 것이 좋다.

---

59) <extension>과 동의어이다.

60) G.S.M (Grams for Square Meter) – 평방미터 당 그램 수 = 종이의 질량, 즉 종이의 질

61) 라인 토탈을 합한 금액

Part 4 Final Draft

Pineup Corporation
579 Kemmons Drive Louisville KY, 13567[62)]
Phone: 585-123-4455 Fax: 585-123-4457
Website: www. pineupcorporation.com

Fax

From: Carol Burton, Director of Pineup Corporation
Fax: 585-123-4457
Phone: 585-123-4455
Date: May 6, 2022

To: Ms. Sharon Kim, Assistant Manager of Woori Enterprise
Fax: 585-914-1234
Phone: 585-914-1237
No. Pages: 1

Subject: Estimate for office paper and 'Especial Stapler'

Please check this below estimate:

Item #	Quantity	Description	Unit Price	Line Total
13590	10	Pineup B4 90 gsm Office Paper (700 sheets)	$10.00	$100.00
22481	10	'Especial Stapler' with the company logo (with 2,000 staples)	$4.50	$45.00
			Subtotal	$145.00
			VAT Rate	10.00%
			VAT	$14.50
			Total	$159.05

62) 한국식 표기: (우편번호) 13567 켄터키주 루이스빌 Kemmons가 579번지

The final payment will be collected before providing you with the goods in this quote.

To accept this quote, please sign here and fax me at 585-123-4457:

Carol Burton

Carol Burton
Pineup Corporation

THANK YOU FOR YOUR BUSINESS

Part 5 무역거래에서 계약이 성사되는 절차

일반적으로 무역거래에서 계약이 성사되기까지의 과정을 살펴보면 상호 간 거래 의사를 확인하고 의견을 교환한 후 합의점을 찾아 계약서를 작성하는 수순을 밟는다. 이때 간과해서 안 될 것은 무역이라는 상행위는 당사자 간 합의에 의한 것이라서 경우에 따라 계약을 체결하는 과정에서 필요한 문서의 순서가 바뀌거나 생략되기도 한다는 점이다. 그 과정에서 보편적으로 통용되는 문서들은 다음과 같다.

1. Estimate (Quote = Quotation) (견적서)

→ 구매자의 요청에 따라 판매자가 물건의 단가와 공급가격을 알려주는 서류이다.

2. Proforma Invoice (= PI) (견적송장) – 생략가능

→ 견적서 내용과 유사하지만 결재수단이나 수수료 등 제반 비용에 대해 보다 상세하게 기재를 하는 차이가 있다. 또한 해당 물품의 가격 및 수량과 관련하여, 더 이상 변경할 수 없다는 법적 구속력을 갖기도 하는데 구매자와 판매자가 서로 잘 아는 경우에는 이를 생략할 수 있다.

3. Purchase Order (발주서)

→ 구매자가 판매자에게 상품을 보내 달라고 주문하는 서류로서 '구매주문서'라고도 부른다.

4. Offer Sheet (매도 확약서) – 생략가능

→ 발주서를 받은 판매자가 판매조건, 예를 들어 가격이나 운송비 등 기타 제반 비용에 대해 다시 확인하는 서류이다. 견적송장의 내용과 실질적으로 일치되는 경우가 많기 때문에 변경사항이 없는 경우에는 이를 생략할 수 있다.

5. Invoice (송장)

→ 판매자가 물건을 선적하고 구매자에게 보내는 청구서이다.

1. 견적서 Estimate, Quote, Quotation

판매자가 구매자에게 물건의 단가와 공급가격을 미리 알려주는 문서이다. 구매자가 견적서를 받고 가격에 만족하여 구매를 결정하면 서명을 하여 회신한다.

<견적서 양식 샘플>

YOUR LOGO HERE

QUOTE

Company Name
Company Slogan

Street Address, City, ST ZIP Code
Phone Phone Fax Fax
Email

INVOICE # NO.
DATE: DATE

EXPIRATION DATE DATE

TO Contact Name
Company Name
Street Address
City, ST ZIP Code
Phone
Customer ID No.

SALESPERSON	JOB	PAYMENT TERMS	DUE DATE
		Due on receipt	

QTY	DESCRIPTION	UNIT PRICE	LINE TOTAL
		SUBTOTAL	
		SALES TAX	
		TOTAL	

Quotation prepared by: ____________________

This is a quotation on the goods named, subject to the conditions noted below: Describe any conditions pertaining to these prices and any additional terms of the agreement. You may want to include contingencies that will affect the quotation.

To accept this quotation, sign here and return: ____________________

THANK YOU FOR YOUR BUSINESS!

2. 견적송장 Proforma Invoice

매매계약이 성사되기 전에 판매자가 구매자에게 발급하는 서류이다. 견적서의 내용과 거의 유사하지만 견적서에 없는 신용장, 결제조건, 수수료 등 모든 제반비용을 포함하고 있기 때문에 견적송장이 발행되면 이에 대한 법적 효력이 발생한다고 할 수 있다. 다시 말해 견적서는 가격 문의에 대한 물건의 단가를 단순히 제시하는 서류로서 법적 효력이 발생하지 않지만, 이와 달리 견적송장은 판매자가 구매자에게 견적송장을 발행하고 구매자가 이를 승인하면 해당 가격과 수량에 대해 법적인 효력이 발생하는 차이가 있다.

<견적송장 실제 샘플>

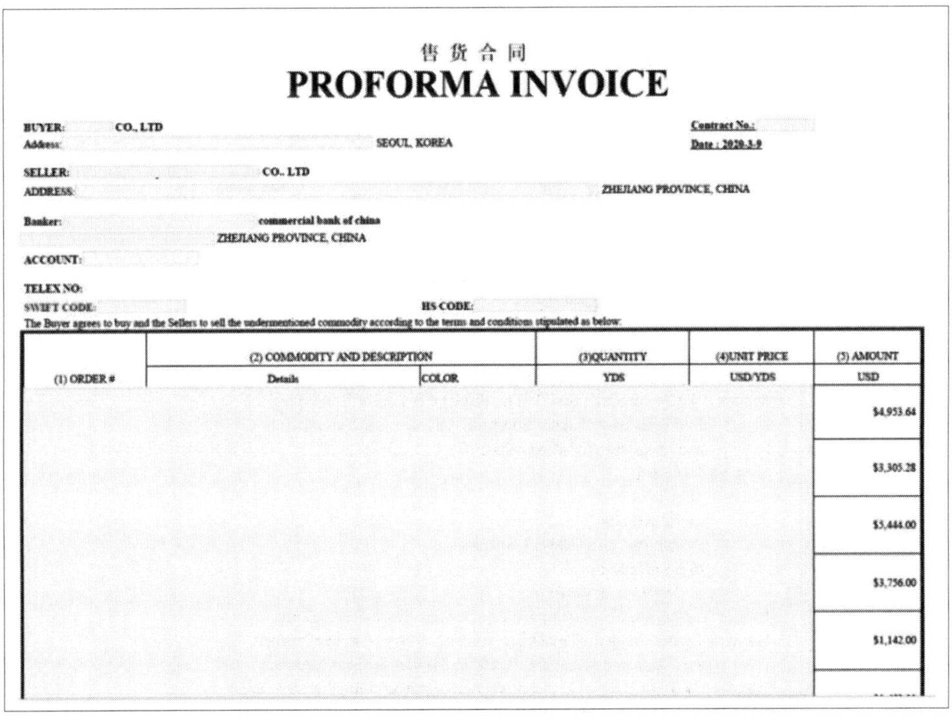

售货合同

PROFORMA INVOICE

BUYER: CO., LTD
Address: SEOUL, KOREA

Contract No.:
Date : 2020-3-9

SELLER: CO., LTD
ADDRESS: ZHEJIANG PROVINCE, CHINA

Banker: commercial bank of china
ZHEJIANG PROVINCE, CHINA

ACCOUNT:

TELEX NO:
SWIFT CODE: HS CODE:

The Buyer agrees to buy and the Sellers to sell the undermentioned commodity according to the terms and conditions stipulated as below:

(1) ORDER #	(2) COMMODITY AND DESCRIPTION		(3)QUANTITY	(4)UNIT PRICE	(5) AMOUNT
	Details	COLOR	YDS	USD/YDS	USD
					$4,953.64
					$3,305.28
					$5,444.00
					$3,756.00
					$1,142.00

3. 발주서 Purchase order

구매자가 판매자에게 상품을 보내 달라고 주문하는 서류로서 '구매주문서'라고도 부른다. 수시로 거래를 하는 기업 간에는 계약서 없이 발주서만 가지고 거래를 하기도 한다.

<발주서 양식 샘플>

ABC CORPORATION
Room 111, Abc B/D, 13 Yeoksam-Dong, Gangnam-gu, Seoul, Korea
Phone: 82-2-123-4567, Fax: 82-2-123-5678 E-mail: abc@abcd.com

PURCHASE ORDER

Date: July. 30, 2019 No.3007.19/AB

The Seller : Gana company
The buyer : ABC CORPORATION
Room 111, Abc B/D, 13 Yeoksam-Dong, Gangnam-gu,
Seoul, Korea

We have a pleasure to confirm our ordering of the following commodities under set forth below:

Description	Quantity	Unit Price(USD)	Amount(USD)
TOTAL:			

- Payment term : by DP in favor of DARA company
- Delivery term : CIF Busan port, Korea
- Delivery time : before Sep. 30, 2019
- Packing : Manufacture's standard and corresponding to transport by sea.
- Inspection : by manufacture to be final
- Remark : 1) 10% contract value shall be deduct if any delay 10-15 days
  2) If delay over 15 days, Buyer has right to refuse the goods and make claim for all damages.
- Shipping documents :
  1) Invoice
  2) Packing List
  3) Manufacture's Quality Certificate
  4) Bill of lading
  5) Certificate of Origin
- Sample : sample must be sent to the Buyer for approval before delivery.
- Warranty : Seller warrants all materials delivered to be free from all defects and that materials conform strictly to the specifications furnished.
- Disputes : All disputes arising in connection with execution of this Purchase Order not reaching an amicable agreement shall be finally settled by arbitration in Seoul, Korea in accordance with the Commercial Arbitration Rules of the Korean Commercial Arbitration Board and the under the Laws of Korea.

This Purchase Order is valid until end of Dec. 2019

Confirm of the Buyer

Confirm of the Seller

4. 매도 확약서 Offer Sheet

발주서를 받은 판매자가 판매조건이나 기타 제반 비용에 대해 다시 확인하는 일종의 확약서이다. 견적송장의 내용과 실질적으로 일치되는 경우가 많기 때문에 변경사항이 없는 경우에는 이를 생략할 수 있다. 판매자가 구매자에게 매도 확약서를 보내면, 이것은 물품에 대한 대금을 지불하라는 의미로 간주할 수 있다.

<매도 확약서 실제 샘플>

TEL : 822

FAX : 822

E-mail : .com

OFFER NO.

REF.NO.

REG.NO.	
DATE	2020-03-12
사업자등록 (납세)번호	

SongPa Gu, Seoul, Korea

FIRM OFFER

MESSRS. CO.,LTD

We are pleased to offer you the undermentioned goods on the terms and conditions described as follows;

Origin	INDONESIA	Validity	
Shipping Port	INDONESIA	Packing	
Manufacturer		Destination	GUATEMALA
Delivery(Shipping Date)	APR 2020(LSD-4/30)		

Payment : (By an irrevocable L/C [V] at sight

) in favor of;

[ ] days from B/L date (Shipper's Usance)

Supplier

– INDONESIA

5. 송장 Invoice

판매자가 물건을 선적한 후 구매자에게 보내는 대금 청구서로서 관세부과의 자료로 활용된다.

<송장 실제 샘플>

.EN

Customer Service: Tel: +65 6578 Fax: +65 6482
Singapore orders : sg.customer.order@ .com
Other enquiries : Singapore.Customer.Service@ .com

Warehouse: Pioneer Hub
15 Pioneer Walk, #06-
Singapore
Tel: +65 6578 Fax: +65 6268

ompany Registration Number : 199800
ST Registration Number : 19-98005

TAX INVOICE

TAX INVOICE NO : 11001702-30
TAX INVOICE DATE : 5/09/2011
PAGE : 1

BILL TO:
300025
CO., LTD
MR. M. J. KHIL
WONJU MEDICAL INDUSTRY PARK
MUNMAK,WONJU-SI KANGWON-DO
220- KOREA
South Korea

SHIP TO :
CO., LTD.
MR M. J. KHIL
WONJU MEDICAL INDUSTRY PARK
MUNMAK,WONJU-SI KANGWON-DO
220- KOREA
South Korea
TEL : 8270 7092 FAX : 822 542

SALES ORDER NO	ORDER DATE	CREDIT TERMS	SHIP VIA	EX SINGAPORE WAREHOUSE
825718	3/10/2011	90 DAYS	UPS	T

STOMER PURCHASE ORDER NO : MNT10310-001

NE NO	PRODUCT CODE	PRODUCT DESCRIPTION	QUANTITY	UOM	UNIT PRICE	EXTENSION
1	NEL	MODULE SINGLE PCB Origin:CN	60.000	EA	8.650	17384.00
2	DOC	SENSOR/PATIENT CABLE10' Origin:CN	60.000	EA	0.000	4800.00
3	100A	ADULT DIGIT Origin:MX	50.000	EA	0.000	3200.00
		Subtotal				25384.00
		Grand Total	480.000	FOB	USD	25384.00

<송장 양식 샘플>

INVOICE

Date: ____________________

Invoice No: ____________________

1. ABC Pte Ltd
2. (UEN 199800515M)
3. No. 29 Ang Mo Kio
4. Industrial Park 2, #04-01
5. Singapore 569507
6. Tel : 65-6489 0100
7. Fax : 65-6489 0300

Bill To	Ship To
Company Name	Company Name
Address Country Code — Postal	Address Country Code — Postal
Tax ID / VAT No.	Tax ID / VAT No.
Contact Person	Contact Person
Tel No.	Tel No.
Email	Email

No	Item Code	Product Description	HS Code	Country of Origin	Quantity	UOM	Unit Value	Total Value

Additional Comments	Invoice Line Total	
	Discount/Rebate	
	Invoice Sub-Total	
	Freight Charges	
Declaration Statement	Insurance	
	Others (Specify Type)	
	Invoice Total Amount	
	Currency Code	
Shipper Signature	Title	Date

Total Number of Packages	
Total Weight (indicate LBS or KGS)	

Answers

Fundamental Exercises pp18 ~20

1. Lake **Louise** in Canada is a beautiful place to visit.
2. Tom is Korean but Jane is **Japanese**.
3. **They** will bring a pen, a bottle of water, and an eraser.
4. I was born on **Saturday,** May 15th, 1966.
5. We **studied** English very hard last night.
6. The teacher visited many **churches** yesterday.
7. **That** boy **goes** to the mountain every morning.
8. There are many **buses** on the street.
9. I went to the city, **Incheon,** a few years ago, but from now on, I will try to visit many **cities**.
10. I saw many **monkeys** at the zoo in **India**.
11. They brought some fruits**:** **an** apple and a few **mangoes**.

*** 보충설명

'some fruits' 다음에 콜론(:)이 아니라 쉼표(comma)를 찍으면 틀린 문장이 된다.

They brought some fruits: an apple and a few mangoes. (O)
They brought some fruits, an apple and a few mangoes. (X)

두 번째 문장, 즉 <They brought some fruits, an apple and a few mangoes.>가 틀린 이유는 'an apple and a few mangoes'가 fruits의 종류를 열거한 것이기 때문이다.

⬇

** 원어민 설명 :The sentence "They brought some fruits, an apple and a few mangoes" is incorrect because "an apple and a few mangoes" are categorized as fruits, and the way the sentence is written implies something like this: The guests brought some fruits. The fruits they brought include an apple and a few mangoes.
This is why a colon is more appropriate for the way that sentence is written.

Another example of where a colon would be more appropriate would be something like this.
→ Many items were purchased for the party: balloons, paper plates, napkins, and extra cups.

For the above sentences to be correct, with commas, they should be re-written like this:

Examples:

→ They brought an apple, some mangoes, and bananas.
→ They brought some fruits including an apple, some mangoes, and bananas.

→ Many items were purchased for the party including balloons, paper plates, napkins, and extra cups.
→ They purchased balloons, paper plates, napkins, and extra cups to prepare for the party.

11-① I ate breakfast, drank tea, and washed the dishes.

> ** 원어민 설명 :
> Correct with a comma:
> → I ate breakfast, drank tea, and washed the dishes.
> Correct with a colon:
> → This morning I did many things: ate breakfast, drank tea, and washed the dishes.

12. The coworker met **an** honest and pretty lady.
13. The janitor left **an** umbrella in his car.
14. The professor is writ**ing** a letter to his friend in France.
15. That leaf growing in this garden is **an** herb.
16. My colleague was satis**fied** with the result of the report.
17. Jeniffer stop**ped** working at this restaurant as a part-time job.
18. The secretary omit**ted** to copy the back page of the newspaper.
19. Today is March 1, 2022. (in 생략)
20. When I go to work, I prefer taking public transportation. (부사절 다음에 쉼표)

2장 Fundamental Exercises p38

1. **Hello,** my name is **Kim, Hyomi, and** my major is **Chinese.**
 = **Hello,** my name is **Hyomi Kim, and** my major is **Chinese.**
 = **Hello,** my name is **Hyomi Kim, and I major in Chinese.**
2. ③ did not have anything
3. in (with)
4. **As a result**, I chose a university department related to China.
 = **Therefore,** I chose a university department related to China.
5. When I was in **contact** with the Chinese people at restaurants and tourist attractions, it was not easy to speak Chinese, but **it was fun.**

Fundamental Exercises p57

1. Knowing that I could seem too authoritative, I am always trying to be more thoughtful, to grow and expand my relationships, and **to understand** other people's situations.
 = Because I know that I could seem too authoritative, I am always trying to be more thoughtful, to grow and expand my relationships, and **to understand** other people's situations.
2. ③ 추진력
3. I **endeavoured** to listen to every student's opinion and felt rewarded **for** making a better campus.
4. ④ 세 명 이상의 친구들
5. ③ in order not to

Fundamental Exercises p78

1. My motto is "**Do** it right the first time, with responsibility".
2. ③ I used to be told that I was too meticulous, but that characteristic helped me to focus.
3. ③ had
4. ④ 조건
5. that

3장 Fundamental Exercises p104

1. ③ Block Form
2. ② sexual orientation
3. out of school
4. ④ Best regards,
5. +82 – 10 – 1234 – 5678

Fundamental Exercises p122

1. 온라인 미디어와 관련해서
2. to
3. majoring in marketing
4. ② that

> **** 원어민 설명:**
> 문법적으로 보았을 때 위 문장에서 우리가 사용할 수 있는 관계대명사로는 <that>과 <which> 둘 다 가능하지만, 이와 달리 북미 현지인들은 <which>가 아니라 <that>만 사용한다고 한다.

5. ④ 모든 문제를 해결하다.

5장 Fundamental Exercises p146

1.

학력	2000년 3월 세종고등학교 입학
	2001년 9월 보문고등학교로 전학
	2003년 2월 보문고등학교 졸업

→ **Education:** Sejong High School – attended March 2000 to September 2001
Bomun High School – September 2001 to February 2003

1-①

학력	2015년 3월 협성대학교 입학
	2019년 2월 협성대학교 졸업

→ **Education:** Hyupsung University – March 2015 to February 2019

2.

자격 및 특기사항	토익 850점 취득

→ **Qualifications and Skills:** Scored 850 on the Toeic

3.

자격 및 특기사항	컴퓨터: Adobe와 Excel에 능숙

→ **Qualifications and Skills:** Computer – Proficient in Adobe Software and Excel
= Computer – Proficient with Adobe Software and Excel

⬇

**** 참고: 'fluent' 와 'proficient' 차이**

일반적으로 언어 능력(수준)을 표현할 때 주로 <fluent>나 <proficient>를 사용하고, 기술(skill) 능력(수준)을 표현할 때는 주로 <proficient>을 사용한다.

외국어 구사능력 기준과 관련하여, **<fluent>**는 원어민에 가까운 업무 관련 작문, 독해 및 회화가 가능한 유창한 수준을 말하고, **<proficient>**는 업무 관련 문서를 읽고 이해하며 영문 이메일을 작성할 수 있는 수준을 말한다. 또한 **<basic>**은 간단한 일상회화가 가능한 수준을 말한다. 이에 대한 원어민의 시각은 다음과 같다:

For languages, you can say "fluent", or proficient in English and Japanese, however, it is more common to refer to languages using **"fluent"** instead of "proficient". Also, "fluent" and "proficient" have slightly different meanings.

<Fluent> means that you are extremely good at the language and are unlikely to make errors with translation, speaking, reading, and writing. **<Proficient>** means that you are very good at the language but you are not able to call yourself "fluent" because there might be something in the language that you are still learning.

For skills, you normally would use the word **"proficient"** instead of fluent.

4.

면허 및 자격증	2010년 10월 운전면허 (1종 대형)_

→ 한국식 표현 :

License and Certificate: Driver's License, 1st Class (Large)[63] - October 2010

** 참고: **Korean Driver's License** (한국 운전면허)

1종 대형 (버스)	Driver's License, 1st Class (Large)
1종 보통 (승합차)	Driver's License, 1st Class (Ordinary)
2종 보통 (승용차)	Driver's License, 2nd Class (Ordinary)
2종 소형 (오토바이)	Driver's License, 2nd Class (Small)

63) Class는 "classification"의 줄임말로서 운전면허의 종류를 뜻한다.

→ 북미식 표현[64]

License and Certificate: Driver's License, Class 2 - October 2010

5.

면허 및 자격증	2015년 3월 무역영어 1급 2017년 5월 유통관리사 2급

→ **License and Certificate:** English for International Trade, Level 1 – March 2015
Distribution Management, Level 2 – May 2017

6.

과외활동	2016년 7월 ~ 2017년 8월 교환학생으로 UCLA 방문

→ **Activities:** Exchange student at UCLA - July 2016 to August 2017
= Attended (Visited) UCLA as an exchange student - July 2016 to August 2017

7.

과외활동	2017년 3월 ~ 2018년 2월 캐나다에서 영어연수

→ **Activities:**

Attended the English training program in Canada – March 2017 to February 2018.
= Participated in an English training program in Canada – March 2017 to February 2018
= English training program attendee/student/participant in Canada – March 2017 to February 2018

6장 Fundamental Exercises p174

1. Clearness (명확성)
2. Conciseness (간결성)
3. ② recipient's address 밑에

64) 캐나다 운전면허 종류:

In BC in Canada, **there are Class 7 licenses for Learner drivers, and Novice (New) drivers.** Once you are no longer considered "new" or "novice" then you can move to Class 5 license, which is to drive a regular car. **Class 1 to 4** is for **commercial drivers,** and **it would depend on what type of vehicle you are driving**... freight truck, bus, taxi, etc... they are all different classes of licenses.

This is specific in British Columbia. **https://en.wikipedia.org/wiki/Driver%27s licences in Canada.** So I would have a Driver's License, **Class 5.**

If you are a **new driver**, it would be a Driver's License, **Class 7.**

If you drive a **commercial heavy truck**, it would be a Driver's License, **Class 3.**

→ A commercial heavy truck is classified as a truck with more than 4 wheels. A class 3 license is also for someone who drives a tow truck.

If you drive **buses**, it would be a Driver's License, **Class 2.**

If you drive **semi-trailer trucks**, it would be a Driver's License, **Class 1.**

4. ② recommend, for

5. block format

7장 Fundamental Exercises p193

1. This is a **self-service** restaurant, so you will need to get your water from the counter.

2. USB stick = memory stick

3. ③ department of administration

4. **I am** Namyeob Hwang, responsible for the DBM products in the department of marketing at IBT.
   = **This is** Namyeob Hwang, responsible for the DBM products **at** the department of marketing at IBT.

5. ④ I was referred to you by Ms. Namyeob Hwang of the Samjin Group.

8장 Fundamental Exercises p212

1. ④ 숨은 참조

2. When we received the order yesterday, 70 cartons of milk arrived in good condition but the **remaining** 30 cartons had an expiration date of May 19.

3. However, we discovered that the **expiration date of** the 30 cartons of milk among them had already expired. **(O)**
   However, we discovered that the **expiration date for** the 30 cartons of milk among them had already expired. **(△)**

4. 저희 베이커리는 가장 신선한 유제품만을 사용하는 것에 자부심을 가지고 있기 때문에

5. ③ we faced a delay in production of our most popular Pretzels

9장 Fundamental Exercises p223

1. sending

2. ③ I really appreciate your inviting me to the job interview.

3. Thank you for helping me with my homework.
   = Thank you for helping with my homework.
   = I appreciate your helping me with my homework.
   = I appreciate your helping with my homework.

4. during my visit at your factory.

5. **Should** there be **anything** you may need from me, please feel **free** to contact me at any time.

10장 Fundamental Exercises p244

1. ③ for not supplying

2. about, in regards to, regarding

3. a lot of (much), on

4. However, I hope that you can still **trust** me.

5. I promise to do everything I can to make it up to you.

11장 Fundamental Exercises p258

1. ② Reference
2. ③ 3 (inclusive of the fax cover)
3. ③ Our travel agency would like to make reservations for twenty five double rooms for six nights from June 9 to 14 inclusive.
4. I **would** appreciate confirmation of the **availability** of the rooms and a quote as soon as possible.
5. ③ area code

황남엽

숙명여자대학교 영어영문학, 숙명여자대학교 영어영문학 박사
현) 협성대학교 글로벌 통상문화학과 교수

연구논문으로 침묵의 이야기를 통한 단절의 해소: 『버섯들의 합창』과 『오바상』, 가족사 탐색을 통한 화자의 성적(sexual) 독립: 『잔월루』와 『타마린드 멤』, "Sex Talk" and the Power of Discourse in Aurora Leigh, 그리고 The Search for the Ideal Female Gender Identity in the Victorian Age: Aurora Leigh and The Awakening 등이 있다.

바로 쓸 수 있는 **비즈니스 영작문**

초판 1쇄 발행 _ 2022년 12월 30일

저 자 · 황 남 엽
발행인 · 정 현 걸
발 행 · 신 아 사
인 쇄 · 대명프린팅
주 소 · 서울특별시 은평구 통일로 59길 4 (2층)
전 화 · (02) 382-6411 팩스 · (02) 382-6401
홈페이지 · www.shinasa.co.kr
E-mail · shinasa@daum.net
출판등록 · 1956년 1월 5일 (제 9-52호)

ISBN 979-11-92428-38-3 (93740)

정가 18,000 원